Northwest Birds
in
Winter

Dedication

For my mother, Lona Barker Contreras, and all of her ancestors

Northwest Birds
in
Winter

Alan Contreras
illustrated by Ramiel Papish

 Oregon State University Press
Corvallis, Oregon

Library of Congress Cataloging-in-Publication Data
Contreras, Alan, 1956-
   Northwest birds in winter / Alan Contreras ; illustrated by Ramiel Papish.
      p. cm.
   Includes bibliographical references and index.
   ISBN 0-87071-425-2 (pbk : alk. paper)
   1. Birds—Northwest, Pacific. 2. Birds—Wintering—Northwest, Pacific. 3. Birds—Northwest, Pacific—Geographical distribution. 4. Birds—Northwest, Pacific—Geographical distribution—Maps.
I. Title.
QL683.N75C65 1997
598'.09795—dc21   97-26736
                                                        CIP

Oregon State University Press
101 Waldo Hall
Corvallis OR 97331-6407
Phone 541-737-3166 • Fax 541-737-3170

Preface and Acknowledgements

I have been interested in winter bird distribution for many years and have enjoyed countless Christmas Bird Counts and other winter excursions. Because there is no easy way to extract the status of the region's birds in winter from the many state, provincial, and regional bird books on the market I decided to generate a basic book on winter birds to fill this gap. I appreciate the opportunity provided by OSU Press to bring this publication to a wide audience.

Any book that covers so large a region necessarily extends beyond the knowledge of any one observer or researcher. I appreciate the willing help of many people who provided information and truth-checked early drafts of the text and maps. The commitment of Hendrik Herlyn in revising the text and drawing the first maps was of special note.

The following people deserve special thanks for reviewing drafts and/or providing useful comments and information used in the book: Barbara Begg, Dick Cannings, Tom Crabtree, Gary Davidson, Mike Denny, Phil Mattocks, Craig Miller, Harry Nehls, Tom Rogers, Chris Siddle, Shirley Sturts, Dan Svingen, Chuck Trost, and Terry Wahl. Photo credits are listed with each photo. Special thanks to Jo Alexander, Jeff Grass, and Tom Booth from OSU Press for their patience and confidence in this project.

This is the fourth publication on which I have worked with the talented nature artist Ramiel Papish of Eugene, Oregon. I thank him as always for helping bring these pages to life. Thanks also to Kristi Whalen for creating the final maps.

One reviewer of an earlier draft noted that because I am an Oregon-based observer and writer the book necessarily has a certain Oregon point of view. This is no doubt true, but I hope that I have been able to paint for the most part with a regional brush to allow observers from throughout the northwest to gain some knowledge and pleasure about our winter birds.

This book is not a comprehensive reference to the region's birds. Readers are referred to the major state, provincial, and local publications for more detailed accounts.

Alan Contreras
May 1997

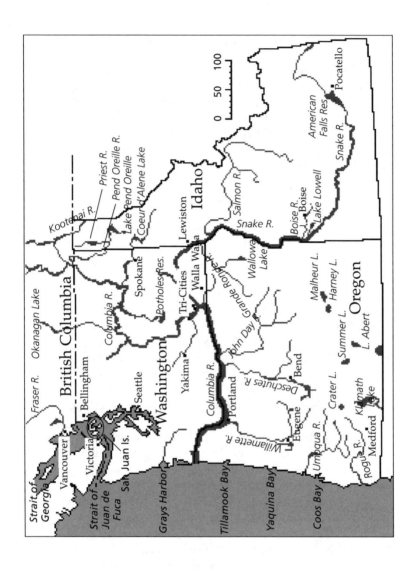

Table of Contents

Introduction and coverage

This book is intended as a guide to the distribution and abundance of birds that winter in the Pacific Northwest region. I treat as "winter" the months of December, January, and February although for some species early December (e.g., southbound Red Phalarope and Bonaparte's Gull) and late February (e.g., northbound Turkey Vulture, waterfowl, Say's Phoebe, Sage Sparrow) involve migration.

For purposes of this book the region is defined as the U.S. states of Oregon, Washington, and Idaho and the southern part of the Canadian Province of British Columbia. Although it would be possible to set boundaries for such a project anywhere that seems appropriate, the region covered by this guide has certain properties that make it particularly appropriate for this project.

First, it contains all of the region between the Rocky Mountains and the Pacific Ocean in northwestern North America except for northern British Columbia, as well as all of the northern Great Basin and almost all of the Columbia-Snake River complex and the Klamath Basin. All of the major inland valleys that are "northwestern" (as distinguished from "Californian") in vegetative character are also included, with the Rogue Valley of Oregon the principal, widely recognized transition point between these two large natural divisions. Finally, the region contains a long, unbroken expanse of the Pacific coastline, including virtually all of the major estuaries between Humboldt Bay, California, and the small estuaries of southern Alaska.

These are natural features that belong together for purposes of reviewing the status of wildlife. There are also natural "breaking points" between the region covered and other regions. The expanse of desert separating the basin lakes of southeastern Oregon and the reservoirs of southern Idaho from the Great Salt Lake and water features of Nevada is one such feature. Another is the expanse of forest (with only small valleys) separating the Rogue Valley from the Central Valley of California. The most obvious natural break is the one provided by the Rocky Mountains, which form the eastern boundary of the region.

The only significant outlier that might have been formally included in the book is the Tule Lake-Lower Klamath Lake area just south of the Oregon border. However, the species that winter there are nearly the same as those that winter on the Oregon side of the border, with the exception of the Plain Titmouse, which is more common in California.

Where to draw the line in British Columbia was of course a somewhat arbitrary decision. I decided to include all of the more temperate valleys (especially the Okanagan and coastal valleys) because they are the natural limit of many species in winter, especially those that require open water. The limit of coverage is set at roughly 50° north latitude and, on Vancouver Island, 126° west longitude. The only exception is that I have tried to include data for the entire Okanagan Valley of British Columbia although the upper part lies above 50°. A few records outside the region (e.g. a winter Swainson's Thrush specimen from northern California, a few records for the Queen Charlotte Islands) are mentioned.

The book is not intended to provide a comprehensive listing of records of birds rare in the region such as eiders, eastern warblers, and the like. That information is provided on some occasions when there are very few records for the entire region or when a species' winter range ends abruptly (e.g., Northern Hawk-Owl) and records from adjacent areas help complete the picture of the species' range.

Winter birds and birding

Observing birds in the Pacific Northwest in winter is both challenging and rewarding. The region's climate ranges from mostly frozen at higher elevations and in the inland valleys of British Columbia and Idaho to quite mild in southwestern Oregon and along the coast. Annual snowfall ranges from over 30 feet in some areas of the Cascade Range of Washington to none on the southern Oregon coast in most years. Precipitation from December to February varies from more than 40 inches in some ranges near the coast to fewer than two inches in parts of southeastern Oregon and southern Idaho.

Into this variety of climates come winter birds. Some are local residents that remain but many are from somewhere else: waterfowl from northern Canada and Alaska, Fox Sparrows from the northern Rocky Mountains, Dunlin from Alaska, Swamp Sparrows from unknown points northeast, Rough-legged Hawks from the tundra, and Gray-crowned

Rosy-Finches from their mountain strongholds here and there. The region also receives winter birds from the south: Great Egrets and White-tailed Kites from California, a few Northern Mockingbirds from unknown southern locales, and some waterfowl moving into the lake basins from higher elevations in northern California. Add to these regular winter birds the surprises—Scott's Oriole in western Washington, Spotted Redshank at the mouth of the Columbia, Hoary Redpolls in the northeast part of the region, late warblers here and there—and the great appeal of winter birding becomes clear.

In the breeding season many birds are territorial and observers must go to many places to see them. In winter many birds concentrate, especially in warmer lowland areas, and a field trip can find amazing densities and species variety in a small area. This is one reason that the Christmas Bird Count, started by the National Audubon Society in 1900, remains a popular birding event and a useful data-generation exercise: it puts the observers where the birds are.

It is helpful for field observers to realize that in winter the birds that we think of as common in the region (e.g. Bullock's Oriole, Chipping Sparrow) are in fact no more likely to be found than physically similar, closely related vagrants and wanderers that come to our region most often in winter (e.g., Hooded Oriole, Clay-colored Sparrow). This necessitates a careful look at birds that seem superficially familiar.

Winter birding is a great joy despite the weather and the fact that many birds are not in their brightest plumage. Who can forget the first time they saw a Bohemian Waxwing in their yard, or came across an Oldsquaw while sifting a flock of scoters? What a special thrill to see the unbelievable flat acceleration of a Merlin as it spots dinner on the far side of a lake, or to see a field full of Rough-legged Hawks sitting on the snow while Snow Buntings move along the fenceline.

We realize that some of the photographs in this book are not of the highest technical quality. Many of them were taken by amateur photographers under difficult circumstances. Nonetheless, they are an important record of the presence of a given bird in winter in the region.

I hope that this book will help you enjoy the region's winter birds by providing a basic overview of the distribution and abundance of each species in the region. Please feel free to call any corrections to my attention.

Finding Birds in Winter

The Northwest has two principal climatic zones in winter: the humid, warmer zone west of the Cascades and the drier, colder, and much larger inland region. Within these zones there are of course microclimates such as the relatively mild Columbia River lowlands of southeastern Washington and the frigid montane regions of the northern Rocky Mountains. These variations have profound consequences for the observer seeking birds in the region in winter.

West of the Cascades open water can be found in abundance and the principal factors governing bird concentrations are food and cover. East of the Cascades the availability of unfrozen water is a third and very significant consideration.

Observers traveling in the region in winter have the opportunity to see many different habitats and to observe distinct sets of birds in each. This section is intended to help observers develop a sense of where to go for the greatest richness of species diversity and also where certain unusual species can best be found.

Coastal regions
British Columbia

Southwestern British Columbia is characterized by a mild climate at a northerly latitude. This combination results in a stunning variety of species to be found in relatively small areas. For example, Christmas Bird Counts (CBC) in this places such as Ladner, Vancouver, and Victoria frequently find in excess of 130 species and sometimes more than 140; this compares to highs in the sixties at similar latitudes in coastal eastern Canada. CBC totals in southwestern British Columbia frequently match and often surpass counts from coastal Washington and Oregon because of good coverage of these relatively mild climatic areas.

Snowy Owls are regular in small numbers and sometimes invade by the score in coastal meadows of southwestern British Columbia. The nearby straits contain some of the continent's largest concentrations of loons, grebes, and waterfowl. Victoria, B.C. holds the all-time North American record for a CBC, over six thousand Ancient Murrelets.Bonaparte's Gulls are more common in winter in this area than elsewhere in the region, and Thayer's Gulls are sometimes present in the thousands in this, their winter stronghold on the continent. On the north side of the Strait of Juan de Fuca the haven of Victoria's Esquimalt Lagoon and the city's many parks provide excellent birding locales.

Best birding sites in winter: Iona Island, Reifel refuge, Esquimalt Lagoon (Victoria), Pitt Meadows, and any location with access to the straits and river valleys.

Washington

Farther south in northern Puget Sound the large estuaries such as Samish Bay and Skagit Bay are not only excellent places to find a great variety of wintering waterfowl but are host to the region's largest flocks of Trumpeter Swans. These open flats are also the most regular sites for annual wintering Gyrfalcons in the region.

The San Juan Islands and the Straits of Juan de Fuca are known for many birds but most people go there for two reasons: the great concentration of Bald Eagles among the islands and the variety and abundance of alcids. Rhinoceros Auklets are most common in central and southern Puget Sound, while Ancient and Marbled Murrelets are common and locally abundant in the open straits. The Strait of Juan de Fuca is also home to a sizable winter population of Pigeon Guillemots. Dungeness Spit is speckled with Snowy Owls in invasion years.

In the urbanized part of Puget Sound such locales as sewage ponds and parks provide good birding, while the ponds and cover available at the Montlake Fill near the University of Washington have produced an astounding variety of birds. Species such as Black-throated Gray Warbler have wintered on the University of Washington campus, and rarities such as Little Gull and Slaty-backed Gull have occurred in Tacoma.

The outer coast of Washington provides both rocky headlands and lush mudflats, with the huge estuaries of Grays Harbor and Willapa Bay offering the best birding. Here such semi-hardy winterers as Willet and Long-billed Curlew join the continent's largest concentrations of Dunlin as well as large numbers of waterfowl and raptors. One Grays Harbor CBC reported ten Merlins and eleven Peregrine Falcons in addition to a Gyrfalcon, which gives an idea of the good conditions for raptor watching on this stretch of coast. The grassy areas along these bays are the northern limit of annual occurrence of White-tailed Kites in the region.

A few Trumpeter Swans now winter annually on the north side of the Columbia River (and some birds are seen in Oregon). **Best birding sites in winter:** Skagit flats, Samish estuary (especially waterfowl and raptors at both these sites), San Juan Islands (eagles and alcids), Montlake Fill (Seattle), Dungeness Spit (seabirds, Gyrfalcon and Snowy Owls), Grays Harbor (waterfowl, shorebirds, raptors), Willapa Bay (waterfowl, shorebirds, raptors), north side of Columbia mouth (shorebirds, waterfowl).

Oregon

The northern Oregon coast is the limit of annual occurrence of Gyrfalcons in the coastal part of the region; single birds reach the South Jetty of the Columbia in most years. Astoria also represents the northernmost limit of frequent reports of Sora in winter, and in some years Cinnamon Teal are present. The Wrentit reaches its northern limit at any season in the area of Fort Stevens State Park.

Birding is generally good along the Oregon coast, with many small bays and the large estuaries at Tillamook, Yaquina Bay, and Coos Bay. Tillamook Bay offers a great variety of waterfowl and, in late winter, Tufted Duck sometimes appears on small ponds along the bay. Dense thickets along the east side of the bay hold the west coast's northernmost concentration of wintering Swamp Sparrows. Yaquina Bay contains large numbers of Brant and the outer estuary is one of the best places to see Oldsquaw and other sea ducks and gulls. King Eider and Ross' Gull are two of the most unusual birds to be found here.

The Oregon coast from Coos Bay southward becomes somewhat drier and supports some species normally associated with California: Snowy Egrets at Coos Bay, Red-shouldered Hawks and Black Phoebes (especially in the Coquille Valley), and Scrub Jays (especially in southern Curry County). Birding is always rich in these areas in winter.

Best birding sites in winter: South Jetty of the Columbia River (Gyrfalcon, Snow Bunting, Snowy Owl), Tillamook Bay (especially waterfowl and raptors), Siletz Bay, Yaquina Bay (waterfowl, raptors, rare passerines), Coos Bay, Bandon/ Coquille Valley (Red-shouldered Hawks, Black Phoebes, waterfowl), Sixes River/Cape Blanco (especially raptors)

Western Interior Valleys

The lowlands of inland southwestern Washington and especially western Oregon provide a wealth of species and high concentrations of some birds. These valleys hold some of the largest winter concentrations of sparrows, Ruby-crowned Kinglets, and thrushes in the region. Golden-crowned Sparrows, a species sought by many visitors to the region, can be especially dense in the blackberry tangles where they join White-crowned Sparrows and the occasional White-throated Sparrow. Another often-pursued species, Mountain Quail, is fairly common in the coast ranges and Cascade foothills along these valleys. In some years Varied Thrushes can be abundant here as well.

The open fields of the central Willamette Valley between Salem and Eugene often provide the best raptor watching in the western interior valleys. Gyrfalcon occurs here almost every year, while Rough-legged Hawks often invade and Prairie Falcons occur every year. Merlins and Peregrine Falcons can often be found, especially near the lakes and marshes.

Inland southwestern Oregon contains the region's chaparral, with such species as California Towhee, Plain Titmouse, and Lesser Goldfinch fairly easy to find. The Rogue Valley represents the northernmost range for the titmouse and the towhee barely extends into the Umpqua drainage. The Rogue Valley also supports small flocks of Lewis' Woodpeckers in winter.

Although there is good birding at many locales in the western interior valleys, excellent public access to a variety of habitats can be found at many of the sites listed below.

Best birding sites in winter: Ridgefield NWR, Vancouver, Washington; Sauvie Island, Oregon; Baskett Slough NWR, Oregon; Finley NWR, Oregon; central Willamette Valley, Oregon (raptors); Fern Ridge Reservoir, Oregon; Plat I Reservoir near Roseburg, Oregon; Rogue Valley, Oregon (Agate Lake, sewage ponds, Table Rocks—local specialties as noted above). Most of these sites are noteworthy for waterfowl and raptors.

East of the Cascades
British Columbia

East of the Cascades many winter birds follow open water. For this reason the best winter birding in the portion of British Columbia covered by this book can be found in the Okanagan Valley. This is the "warm" part of inland B.C. and has certain characteristics in common with the coastal part of the province: a combination of arctic species with those semi-hardy birds that linger in the milder climate of the lake valley. Such birds as Gyrfalcon and Common Redpoll occur here alongside lingering waterfowl. Greater Scaup winter in numbers and goldeneye and other diving ducks remain wherever open water is available. Compared to the coast, the lowlands in this region receive little winter precipitation.

Best birding sites in winter: Okanagan and Osoyoos lakes and adjacent valleys; Lake Kootenay. All are noteworthy for waterfowl and gulls, and especially the Okanagan Valley for raptors.

Washington

Central and eastern Washington are similarly cold and relatively dry, with most precipitation falling as snow in the mountains. Water birds tend to concentrate at lakes such as Lake Chelan, managed sites such as Columbia NWR adjacent to Potholes Reservoir, and along open reaches of the Columbia River and the confluence of its tributaries such as the Walla Walla River and Snake River.

Small birds in this cold, dry part of the region (and throughout most of eastern Oregon and Idaho) can be found in numbers where food and shelter are available, especially in riparian areas and in cities. Even small urbanized areas provide slightly warmer microclimates, access to shelter in ornamental plantings, and of course many bird feeders. Species such as Anna's Hummingbird have wintered or attempted to winter as far north as Wenatchee, Washington, by using feeders.

Eastern Washington—like southeastern British Columbia, northeastern Oregon and much of Idaho—is invaded in most years by flocks of Bohemian Waxwings. These birds are often sought by birders from the western parts of the region, and can most easily be found in ornamental plantings in the region's cities. Other species that move into the eastern part of the region in winter include American Tree Sparrow (found regularly as far southwest as central Washington, central Idaho, and Northeastern Oregon), Common Redpoll (less regular and more irruptive), and Blue Jay (numbers vary, but annual from northern Idaho and northeastern Oregon northward).

Birders also come to the cold northeastern part of the region in search of such genuine rarities as Northern Hawk-Owl (rare to eastern Washington, very rare to northeastern Oregon). Great Gray Owls sometimes move down from their montane haunts to delight visiting birders who sometimes find them in such obvious locations as sitting on roadside fence posts.

Best birding sites in winter: Lake Chelan, Potholes Reservoir/Columbia NWR, Walla Walla River mouth, Snake and Columbia River dams and access points (especially for gulls), urban parks.

Idaho

Northern Idaho offers good birding at lakes such as Pend Oreille and Coeur d'Alene (where gulls, waterfowl, and species such as Red-necked Grebe winter in numbers) and at smaller lakes. Much of the panhandle and the central part of the state is dominated by the Rocky Mountains and several wilderness areas, and winter access is difficult. Away from open water the best birding in this region in winter is usually in towns and cities where feeders and plantings provide food and shelter for passerines. Such "regular" rarities as Blue Jay are most often reported in the region from northern Idaho and nearby eastern Washington and northeastern Oregon.

The more southerly Snake River plain and the valleys extending into the Rockies from the south provide good birding. Lake Lowell at Deer Flat NWR near Nampa provides winter habitat for thousands of waterfowl, and the region to the southeast of Nampa supports scores of raptors at all seasons.

The Snake River valley in general provides a milder climate than the mountains and more northerly regions, and the southeastern part of the state offers good birding at Lake Walcott (Minidoka NWR) and especially at American Falls Reservoir just west of Pocatello. Extreme southeastern Idaho offers such species as Western Scrub-Jay, Pinyon Jay and Plain Titmouse.

Best winter birding: Coeur d'Alene Lake, Mann Lake, Lake Pend Oreille, Snake River valley (especially raptors), Lake

Lowell (waterfowl), Minidoka NWR, American Falls Reservoir (gulls, waterfowl), urban parks.

Oregon

Eastern and central Oregon are similar to the rest of the inland region but have certain distinct characteristics and species. The juniper belt of central Oregon is the northernmost outpost of the Pinyon Jay, which forms large flocks and is fairly common. The lake basins at Malheur NWR, Summer Lake and Upper Klamath Lake support tens of thousands of waterfowl and also represent isolated regular wintering grounds for such species as Virginia Rail, Marsh Wren, Snow Goose, Ross' Goose (Klamath Basin), Ferruginous Hawk (local north to Washington), Sage Sparrow (in mild years), Loggerhead Shrike (local to the Columbia and Snake lowlands). By late February Say's Phoebes are already moving north into this part of the region.

Best winter birding: Columbia River dams (gulls, waterfowl—especially at McNary Dam), Klamath Basin (especially raptors and waterfowl), Wallowa County (raptors and eastern specialties)

Finding Birds in the Region

There are many excellent guides to birding and the status of the region's birds. Visitors should consult the following when planning a trip. Only books in print as of spring 1997 are included.

British Columbia

A Bird Watching Guide to the Vancouver Area. 1993. Vancouver Natural History Society. Site guides, seasonal abundance, information on rarities.

Waterbirds of the Strait of Georgia. 1991. E. C. Campbell, R. W. Campbell, and R.T. McLaughlin. A small field guide with color illustrations and site guides. Covers a small number of species in detail.

Birds of the Okanagan Valley, British Columbia. 1987. Robert A. Cannings, Richard J. Cannings, and Sydney G. Cannings. Royal British Columbia Museum. Not a site guide but perhaps the archetype of regional studies, with maps, photographs and exhaustive detail about the status of each species in this unique part of Canada. Excellent use of CBC data gives a good picture of early winter status.

Birds of British Columbia. Volumes 1 and 2. 1990. Campbell, R., N. Dawe, J. Cooper, G. Kaiser, M. McNall, and I. McT. Cowan. Royal British Columbia Museum. A massive compilation of information including excellent use of CBC data. Not a site guide. Volume 3 was released in 1997.

Washington

Birds of the Tri-Cities and Vicinity. 1991. Howard R. Ennor. Lower Columbia Basin Audubon Society. Covers the area near the Pasco-Richland-Kennewick area of southeastern Washington. Status, some natural history and suggested birding routes with maps.

Birds of Whatcom County. 1995. Terence R. Wahl. Not a site guide but an excellent status book with considerable information on where species can be found. Covers the northwestern part of the state adjacent to mainland British Columbia.

Birding in Seattle and King County. 1982. Eugene S. Hunn. Site guides, status graphs, information on frequently-sought species.

A Birder's Guide to Ocean Shores, Washington. 1994. Bob Morse. Covers some of the best birding areas at Grays Harbor.

Birding in the San Juan Islands. 1987. Mark G. Lewis and Fred G. Sharpe. Suggested birding routes, seasonal bar graphs.

Oregon

The Birder's Guide to Oregon. 1990. Joseph E. Evanich, Jr. Portland Audubon Society. Site guides for the entire state. Also contains information on finding certain sought-after species. Ranks areas by season.

Birds of Oregon. 1994. Jeff Gilligan, Mark Smith, Dennis Rogers and Alan Contreras. Cinclus. A general status book on the state's birds. No site guides.

Birds of Malheur National Wildlife Refuge. 1990. Carroll D. Littlefield. Oregon State University Press. Includes seasonal status. This refuge is the most visited birding site in Oregon.

Birds of Malheur County, Oregon (including the Snake River islands of adjacent Idaho). 1996. Alan Contreras and Robert

R. Kindschy. Not a site guide but has information on the status of birds of far southeastern Oregon and nearby Idaho.

Birds of Northeast Oregon. 1992. Joseph E. Evanich, Jr. Oregon Field Ornithologists. Not a site guide, but an annotated checklist with some seasonal information. Covers Union and Wallowa counties.

A Birder's Guide to the Klamath Basin. 1993. Steven D. Summers. Klamath Basin Audubon Society. Excellent site guides to the Oregon and California part of the basin, with seasonal bar graphs.

Birding the Southern Oregon Coast. 1996. Cape Arago Audubon Society. Covers the southern half of the coast, from Florence to the California line. Site guides and seasonal bar graphs.

Idaho

Birds and Birding routes of the Idaho Panhandle. 1993. Shirley Sturts. Idaho Dept. of Fish and Game. Site guides, excellent maps, suggested routes, seasonal status.

Birds of East-central Idaho. 1992. Hadley B. Roberts. Species accounts, trip guides, status, habitat information. Covers the upper Salmon River valley.

Data Sources

Christmas Bird Count (CBC) data were used extensively in preparing this book. The data base provided by the National Biological Service (NBS) (see below) contains all counts from 1959 to 1988. More recent counts were also used when available.

There are various pitfalls to using CBC data, not the least of which are that the original data contain errors of identification, the published counts include errors of typography, and the NBS data-entry process contains additional errors. At first glance this layer-cake of potential mistakes might seem to render CBC data singularly useless for a serious research project. However, the data have certain advantages.

First, the sheer volume of information is so great that even the errors noted above tend to leach out over time when using a thirty-year-plus database. Second, studies have shown that, given enough data, the CBC shows essentially the same population trends as does the North American Breeding Bird Survey and carefully monitored small-scale winter population studies (see Butcher 1990), thereby providing a certain level of validation for use of the data. Finally, in the Northwest CBCs are widely distributed through almost every habitat except the high mountains (only a couple of counts) and open ocean (the first fully pelagic CBC in the region has been scheduled for Oregon's Heceta Banks in late 1997) and therefore provide adequate data for the great majority of species that winter in the region.

As Butcher (1990) noted in his summary of the use of CBCs for research purposes, "for all its difficulties, the CBC has an impressive record for producing useful analyses of the population dynamics of North American birds." For readers interested in reviewing technical articles regarding the validity and use of CBC data in more detail, I recommend Peterson (1995) on ways to fix erroneous party-hour data; Confer et al. (1979), Falk (1979), and Smith (1979) on the impact of weather, observer effort, and count location; Bock and Root (1981) for an excellent overview of a wide variety of CBC-related issues; and Drennan (1981) on statistical issues and their impact on count validity. Root (1988), an early attempt to map CBC data directly in atlas format, is interesting mainly for the difficulties encountered and has a text of dubious accuracy and little utility. However, it does provide continent-wide maps with useful density information for the more common species.

In addition to the CBC data, publications on the region's birds were used as a source of information. Among these were, for British Columbia, Campbell et al. (1990) and Cannings et al. (1987); for Idaho, Stephens and Sturts (1991) and Sturts (1993); for Oregon, Contreras and Kindschy (1996), Evanich (1992), Fix (1991), Gabrielson and Jewett (1940), Gilligan et al. (1994), Littlefield (1990), and Summers (1993); and for Washington, Jewett et al. (1953), Ennor (1991), Wahl (1995) and Mattocks et al. (1976). The published data of King (1974) and unpublished records of Greg Gillson were especially helpful for pelagic species.

Although I do not emphasize records of rare birds in the book, I used many records provided through the courtesy of the rare bird committees of the region (abbreviated in the text as OBRC and WBRC, Oregon/Washington Bird Record Committee), published actions of these committees, and related compilations of rare bird data in *Murrelet, Oregon Birds, Washington Birds,* and the *Washington Ornithological Society News.*

Note: The Canadian spelling "Okanagan" is used in preference to the U.S. spelling "Okanogan" (except for Washington proper names) because almost all data included are from the Canadian part of the valley, mainly from Cannings et al. (1987), "Birds of the Okanagan Valley, British Columbia," a fine example of what regional ornithology is all about.

The Maps

The dark shaded area on the maps accompanying each account for regularly occurring species is intended to represent *the range in which a species can be found in appropriate habitat on at least 80 percent of day-long trips, or in which the species is found on 80 percent of Christmas Bird Counts over time.* The lighter shade represents regular but less frequent occurrence. Note that some water birds are more widespread east of the Cascades in mild years when open water is available. In some cases where data were limited (e.g., the Columbia River valley between The Dalles, Oregon, and the Walla Walla River mouth, or the mountainous west-central part of Idaho) range maps are extrapolated based on what limited data are available.

The maps are hand-drawn originals converted to computer images, rather than computer-generated from the CBC database. For good density maps for many species generated by computer see the National Biological Survey maps at http://www.mbr.nbs.gov/bbs/cbc.html.

Mapping software is much better than it once was but is still inadequate for mapping distribution where data points are unevenly distributed or where habitat contours are more complex than the software can process. The original maps were prepared by Hendrik Herlyn with subsequent editing by me as a result of checking additional references and from comments from Dick Cannings, Mike Denny, Phil Mattocks, Craig Miller, Shirley Sturts, Dan Svingen, and Chuck Trost.

The maps are intended to show winter ranges only. In many cases breeding ranges differ. For information on breeding ranges see Campbell et al. (1990) for British Columbia, Stephens and Sturts (1991) for Idaho, and breeding bird atlas data in preparation for Oregon and Washington.

How to Interpret the Species Accounts
Abundance Scale

Abundant—Can be found in good numbers (more than 20) on almost all trips.

Common—A few (fewer than 20) found on almost all trips.

Uncommon—A few (fewer than 20) found on only a few trips.

Occasional—Very small numbers (fewer than 10) found on a few trips almost every year.

Rare—Very small numbers (fewer than 10) found on very few trips and seldom every year.

Vagrant—Out of normal range and fewer than five records for the area in winter.

Wanderer—Usually a bird near the edge of its regular range, or that occurs as part of a pattern.

Local—Does not use all apparently suitable habitat, found only in preferred spots.

Most observers will recognize that this scale works better for some families—and sometimes individual species—than for others. The scale is designed for average field birders' use. Researchers working with Soras or Northern Saw-whet Owls may well find ten times more birds than I would. Christmas count tallies for species such as White-tailed Kite and Tundra Swan probably approach actual representation of all the birds present in some circles, while counts of rails and owls are essentially useless except as indicators of the species' presence or absence. Species such as wrens and towhees fall in between. Terry Wahl noted the distinction quite clearly in his recent book *Birds of Whatcom County* as the difference between a *census* (of all swans actually in the circle) and a *sample* (of "small brown birds" such as Winter Wrens in the circle).

Abundance information given in the species accounts refers to the bird's presence in appropriate habitat; it does not reflect the presence of Sharp-shinned Hawks in sage desert or of Northern Pintail in pine forests.

Definitions

Cascade Mountains—The range by that name in Oregon, Washington, and extreme southern British Columbia. Also used for convenience in this book to include the Lillooet Range in southwestern British Columbia.

Columbia-Snake system—Usually, the valleys or waters of the Columbia and Snake rivers north to northern Washington and east to eastern Idaho. I do not use this term to include the Columbia in British Columbia.

Klamath Basin—The area around Upper Klamath, Lower Klamath and Tule lakes, in Oregon and California.

Outer coast—The coastline facing the Pacific Ocean in Oregon and Washington and along the western shore of Vancouver Island, B.C.

Puget Sound—The area encompassing the San Juan Islands and waters to the south and east, north roughly to Bellingham, WA.

Straits—The Straits of Georgia and Juan de Fuca except as noted.

Western interior valleys—The most common usage is for the Willamette, Umpqua and Rogue River valleys of western Oregon, including the Columbia River lowlands from Troutdale, OR, roughly to Kelso, WA, and the region of southwestern Washington around Chehalis except as noted.

How to read the CBC Trend boxes

The data shown in the CBC Trend boxes have been provided by the National Biological Service and represent all counts conducted in the region in the period 1959-88. For some species the NBS could not provide usable data. This includes counts held in northern British Columbia outside the scope of this book. Only a few counts in the region have operated that long, but data from those that have operated for shorter periods are included. The appendix provides a more complete description of the data and appropriate limits on their use.

Location	Trend	Circles	Birds/100 ph
BC	7	34	0.91
WA	3.5	35	1.24
OR	2.1	34	1.33
ID	1.1	12	0.19
ALL	1.4	1398	1.97

From left to right, the columns in the above fictitious example have the following meanings.

Location—The four political entities covered in the book have separate trend data displayed. The "ALL" figures represent all CBC data for the continent, not just the Northwest, thus the data for, e.g., Idaho, can be compared to that for the continent. When there is insufficient data for a species in a given political entity, e.g. Yellow-billed Loon in Oregon, no numbers appear. Unfortunately the NBS could not provide data for some relatively common species owing to technical difficulties.

Trend—The apparent increase or decrease in the species, shown as *percent annual change*. This cannot be used to calculate an overall trend simply by multiplying by the number of years involved. See appendix for details.

Circles—The number of CBC circles (counts held during the period, whether or not they are still active) used to generate the data shown.

Birds/100 ph—Relative abundance of the species, displayed as birds per 100 party-hours. All methods of displaying CBC data have certain drawbacks, but party-hours are the most widely used. See the introduction and appendix for a discussion of the uses and limitations of CBC data.

A Note on Taxonomy

The 41st Supplement to the AOU Checklist appeared in July 1997, while this book was in proofs. Species and family names were changed accordingly, and the layout of the book was amended to reflect the rearrangement of families.

Order GAVIIFORMES
Family Gaviidae

Red-throated Loon
Gavia stellata

The Red-throated Loon is uncommon to locally common along the coast, in the straits, Puget Sound, and the lower Columbia estuary. It is most abundant in northern Puget Sound and the straits, where counts in the hundreds are common and it is often the most common loon. It is occasional to rare on lakes and the  largest rivers away from the coast, and most often seen on the Columbia River and on lakes west of the Cascades. This species is progressively rarer away from the coast, but there are a few records from isolated locations as far inland as northern and southwestern Idaho. It is very rare in eastern Washington and Oregon.

Abundance varies from year to year even at favored coastal locales, where CBC tallies can range from a few birds to hundreds from one year to the next. This loon uses a variety of feeding areas from the open ocean to small backwaters upriver to the edge of tidewater.

Location	Trend	Circles	Birds/100 ph
BC	-0.7	28	1.65
WA	1.6	23	2.26
OR	0.7	14	1.43
ALL	-1.4	376	7.82

Pacific Loon
Gavia pacifica

Abundance varies widely by year and location, but this is usually the least common loon (except for the rare Yellow-billed) at most Northwest coast locations. It is most abundant in the straits (especially Active Pass, B.C.) and northern Puget Sound, where it is sometimes the most common loon, but it can be rare away from prime feeding grounds. It has occurred at lakes and on the Columbia River inland to eastern British Columbia (rare), Washington, Oregon, and (rarely) Idaho. In eastern Oregon, eastern Washington, and Idaho, this species is found somewhat more frequently than Red-throated Loon, and is regular in small numbers on the Columbia River of central and southeastern Washington (M. Denny, personal communication). Generally seen on the ocean or in lower estuaries, it does not usually venture as far upriver as Common and Red-throated Loons. It is more likely to be seen in numbers on the ocean than are other loons.

This species sometimes forms rafts of a dozen or more birds, especially in late winter and spring. Although other loons do this, it seems to occur more frequently among Pacific Loons. CBC numbers range from one or two to over a hundred birds, with considerable variation from year to year.

Note: The Arctic Loon (*Gavia arctica*) has not been reliably reported from the Northwest, but it has been reported from California, so observers should be alert to the possibility of its occurrence here.

Location	Trend	Circles	Birds/100 ph
BC	5.0	28	5.67
WA	6.7	22	9.43
OR	1.9	15	1.15
ALL	5.5	154	2.10

Common Loon
Gavia immer

This is the most widespread loon in winter in the Northwest, occurring on both salt and fresh water, and regularly on the Columbia River to eastern Oregon and Washington. Except from northern Puget Sound northward, it is usually the most common loon in most situations, though in central Oregon the Pacific Loon is more regular in winter.

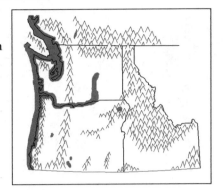

Numbers of this species do not fluctuate as widely at given locations as do numbers of the smaller loons. It is common on the ocean, estuaries, and large lakes. It is occasional inland and east of the Cascades and appears on lakes and reservoirs in northern and southeastern Idaho when they are not frozen.

Location	Trend	Circles	Birds/100 ph
BC	0.1	39	3.11
WA	1.5	31	1.70
OR	0.3	22	1.11
ALL	0.7	998	1.09

Common Loons

Yellow-billed Loon
Gavia adamsii

This loon is occasional in salt water south to southern British Columbia (annual) and Washington (three to five records/year), progressively more rare south along the Oregon coast. One or two birds are seen annually in winter in Puget Sound, and in recent years the species has been reported almost annually at the mouth of the Columbia River, with more than one bird sometimes present. It has been reported on the Oregon coast south to Bandon.

It is generally seen in the shallow part of estuaries and bays; this is not usually an ocean loon in this region in winter.

This species seems more regular now than it was twenty years ago, but this may be an artifact of observer awareness and coverage. There are a handful of records of migrants inland, especially from the Okanagan Valley, BC, where the species is found almost annually, and even to southwestern Idaho (eleven records statewide), so observers away from the coast should be alert for the species, especially in the northern part of the region. There are two inland winter records from Grant County, WA.

Location	Trend	Circles	Birds/100 ph
BC	-0.1	17	0.04
ALL	-0.8	38	0.04

Order PODICIPEDIFORMES
Family Podicipedidae

Pied-billed Grebe
Podilymbus podiceps

This grebe is common to locally abundant in some years on coastal lakes; common to uncommon inland throughout the region, limited primarily by the availability of open water. It is rare in British Columbia north of the region covered by this book.

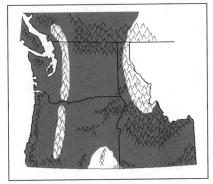

It prefers freshwater locations but will use brackish and occasionally salt water, though it does not usually use the ocean at all. It prefers lakes, ponds, slow-moving rivers, and backwaters.

Numbers range from a few at higher, colder locations to over two hundred on coastal CBCs, and vary somewhat from year to year. CBC trend data show a slight increase over time.

Location	Trend	Circles	Birds/100 ph
BC	0.7	34	0.91
WA	3.5	35	1.24
OR	2.1	34	1.33
ALL	1.4	1398	1.97

Pied-billed Grebe

Horned Grebe
Podiceps auritus

This species is common to locally abundant at coastal locations, where dozens of birds often congregate at favored spots. Numbers up to the hundreds can be found at some locations along the coast. It is uncommon to occasional inland but reported regularly on lakes, reservoirs, and the largest rivers. It is rare in winter in most of eastern Oregon (increasing from migration during February) and southern Idaho; uncommon to common in the Idaho panhandle and on the Columbia River from northern Oregon through southeast Washington and on the lakes of southern British Columbia.

This species is common on both salt and fresh water in winter, and is often seen with other species such as Western or Red-necked Grebes on the ocean.

Location	Trend	Circles	Birds/100 ph
BC	-1.3	39	8.28
WA	1.5	30	9.32
OR	0.5	24	1.19
ALL	-1.4	991	2.11

Red-necked Grebe
Podiceps grisegena

The Red-necked Grebe is uncommon to occasional at most coastal locales, but forms rafts of scores of birds at some locations in some years. It is locally common on the Washington coast, but can be quite hard to find away from favored areas. It is most often seen in the lower parts of estuaries and in protected waters such as the lee side of islands and sheltered coves on the open coast, but is also seen on the open ocean. It is most often seen singly or in small groups of two to five birds. CBC data show an increase over time.

This species is rare away from salt water in Oregon, even on the Columbia River. It is also rare in eastern Oregon, eastern Washington, and inland British Columbia except at larger lakes and locally on the Columbia River, where it is occasional (in most of the region) to locally common in southern British Columbia. It is not reported in winter from Idaho except from large lakes in the panhandle, where it is uncommon to common.

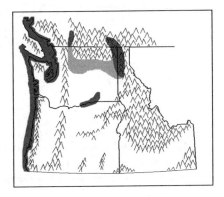

Location	Trend	Circles	Birds/100 ph
BC	0.9	39	2.67
WA	3.0	26	6.40
OR	4.5	15	0.24
ALL	1.7	353	1.25

Eared Grebe
Podiceps nigricollis

On the coast this grebe is uncommon and somewhat local in sheltered waters of British Columbia and Puget Sound, with flocks rarely numbering more than twenty birds. In coastal Oregon and Washington it is occasional and local, and is often absent from CBCs. CBC data show a slight regionwide decrease, but the relatively small number of birds involved limits the utility of the data.

Inland it is occasional to rare west of the Cascades, mainly on large bodies of water and at such locales as sewage ponds. It is rare east of the Cascades except in mild years at Klamath Lake and Lake Abert, OR, but can appear anywhere when open

Location	Trend	Circles	Birds/100 ph
BC	-5.9	21	0.55
OR	-0.2	23	0.21
WA	-6.1	27	2.32
ALL	-1.8	502	16.47

water permits. Eared Grebes are occasional to rare in winter farther inland to southeastern Idaho and southern British Columbia on larger lakes and reservoirs when open water permits. It is very rare in southeast Washington and northeast Oregon.

It is sometimes seen alone, but often with groups of Horned Grebes. It prefers shallow sheltered waters, and is rare on open salt water except in the straits.

Western Grebe
Aechmophorus occidentalis

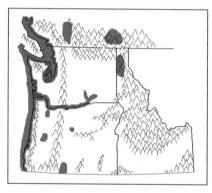

The Western Grebe is common to locally abundant on salt water in winter, with rafts of more than a hundred birds often seen, and several hundred on a CBC not uncommon. Concentrations of over two thousand can be found around the mouth of the Columbia River. In northern Puget Sound and the Straits of Georgia thousands of birds sometimes gather: an all-time Canadian record 15,450 were on the Vancouver CBC in 1969, and 26,230 were at Bellingham, WA, in 1991.

It is common to occasional inland, with birds concentrating at favored sites such as the Columbia River and large lakes and reservoirs north into British Columbia. It is regular in small numbers east to Idaho when lakes remain unfrozen.

This species uses a wide variety of water habitats, including the ocean, estuaries, and fresh water; an occasional bird is seen on medium-sized rivers such as the Willamette.

Clark's Grebe
Aechmophorus clarkii

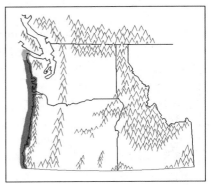

The status of this species is still not clear because most observers did not attempt to distinguish it before the AOU declared it a species in 1983. Also, in winter the facial plumage of this species is sometimes more similar to that of the Western Grebe than in other seasons. It winters in very small numbers (one to five birds) at coastal locations, and at least sometimes inland on large bodies of water. There are two or three recent winter records from eastern Washington and several from eastern Oregon. It is not yet reported in winter in Idaho, but observers there should remain alert for it. There are few winter records for British Columbia. One was at Boundary Bay on December 7-8, 1986, and single birds were at Richmond on January 18, 1987, December 16, 1990, and again on December 15, 1991.

On the coast it appears to favor the deeper parts of lower estuaries over ocean locations, but this may be a result of better observer access.

Order PROCELLARIIFORMES
Family Diomedeidae

Black-footed Albatross
Phoebastria nigripes

This species occurs offshore in winter, but records are few owing to the difficulty of scheduling pelagic trips during winter weather and sea conditions. It is uncommon off British Columbia and, based on limited records, probably uncommon off the rest of the region's coast as well.

The only Oregon CBC record is of two seen off Coos Bay in 1976. There are several additional records in December and January off the Oregon coast. See Sanger (1970, 1972, 1974) for more details of the species' status in the region. Sanger (1974) indicates that the species is more frequently observed off Washington in January than in December.

Laysan Albatross
Phoebastria immutabilis

This species is present in small numbers offshore, but data are limited. It is probably uncommon throughout the offshore region in winter. Two were found about 75 miles west of Vancouver Island on February 27, 1958 (Sanger 1965), and Sanger (1972) treated the species as uncommon far off the region's coast. Two were found about 15 miles west of Coos Bay, OR (outside the CBC circle) on a boat trip run on the 1976 CBC. Two were seen 33 miles west of Newport, OR, on a pelagic trip on January 29, 1994. One was seen by the same boat 20 miles offshore. A high count of thirty was reported off the Washington coast on December 3, 1995. Wahl et al. (1993) treat the species as uncommon in winter off Washington. Sanger (1974) indicates that it is more frequently observed off the Northwest coast in January than in December. See Sanger (1970, 1972, 1974) for more details of the species' status in the region.

Short-tailed Albatross
Phoebastria albatrus

This albatross is extremely rare offshore. One immature was reported on a pelagic trip December 11, 1961, 32 miles west of Yachats, Lincoln County, OR (*Condor* 65:163). One was seen off Tofino, BC, in February 1996, and an immature was off Westport, WA, on January 16, 1993.

Family Procellariidae

Northern Fulmar
Fulmarus glacialis

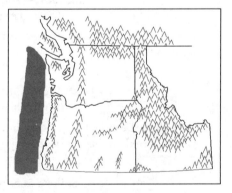

The Northern Fulmar occurs offshore in winter, but abundance is not well known because of the limited number of offshore trips in winter. Based on its relative abundance on the few trips that have generated winter data, it is probably common. National CBC trend data are not especially helpful because of the small number of counts reporting the species.

Sanger (1970) noted many off British Columbia in winter. There are multiple winter records off Washington and Wahl et al. (1993) treat the species as abundant there. Seventy, including white-phase birds, were seen around boats 33 miles west of Newport, OR, on January 29, 1994, but only a few birds were noted by that trip at other offshore locations. Additional research is required in order to determine its true status.

Mottled Petrel
Pterodroma inexpectata

This is a rare wanderer offshore. British Columbia has one winter record, February 24, 1971, off Vancouver Island. There are five winter records for Oregon, four living birds and one washed up dead, all in December. Three of the living birds were seen from boats offshore, while one was at Boiler Bay after a severe windstorm. Three were seen off Washington on December 3, 1995.

Murphy's Petrel
Pterodroma ultima

A possible rare vagrant offshore. Its status is unknown.

Cook's Petrel
Pterodroma cooki

This is a rare vagrant offshore. There is one recent specimen record from Washington on December 12, 1995.

Pink-footed Shearwater
Puffinus creatopus

It is rare in winter offshore. One seen off Westport, WA, in January 1995.

Flesh-footed Shearwater
Puffinus carneipes

There have been no confirmed winter records in the region. One was reported on the 1983 Coos Bay, OR, CBC.

Buller's Shearwater
Puffinus bulleri

There have been no confirmed winter records in the region. One was reported on the 1989 Yaquina Bay, OR, CBC. Another was reported December 11, 1982, off Coos Bay, OR.

Sooty Shearwater
Puffinus griseus

Sooty Shearwaters are considered very rare off British Columbia in winter and are rarely reported on Washington CBCs, while farther south they are more occasional to common in small numbers. This species is often reported from Oregon coastal locations, especially on older CBCs,

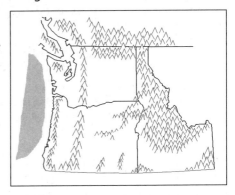

sometimes in the thousands, but many of these are probably actually Short-tailed Shearwaters. Identification problems render CBC data quite suspect.

The paucity of winter pelagic trip data limits a full understanding of the movements of this species, but it is clear that at least a few can be seen off the Northwest coast into December. Most dark shearwaters seen after mid-November are probably Short-tailed Shearwaters.

Short-tailed Shearwater
Puffinus tenuirostris

This is the dark shearwater normally seen off the Northwest coast from mid-November through early winter. It is rare off British Columbia and much more common farther south, with thousands sometimes seen off the Oregon coast in

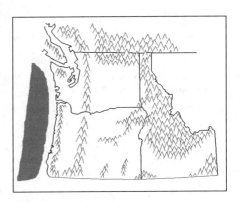

early December when conditions are right. Birds typically come close to shore when storms blow them in or under fog banks or mist.

Although questions about identification cloud the certainty of some records, it is clear from specimens and multiple records over many years that this species is regular, sometimes common, off Oregon during this period. However, they may depart the area by mid-winter: a pelagic trip out of Newport, OR, on January 29, 1994, found no Short-tailed Shearwaters.

Black-vented Shearwater
Puffinus opisthomelas

The only winter record for the region is of a specimen collected in February 1895 off the southern tip of Vancouver Island, BC. There have been late fall records in Oregon.

Family Hydrobatidae

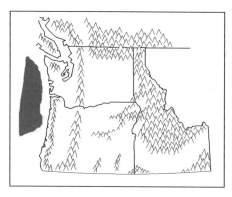

Fork-tailed Storm-Petrel
Oceanodroma furcata

This species is present off the coast and in the Straits of Juan de Fuca in winter, but most birds remain far at sea. Abundance information is therefore limited. Wahl et al. (1993) consider the species rare off British Columbia and Washington. Winter records include a single bird on the Yaquina Bay CBC in 1985; one photographed at Surrey, BC, on January 16, 1984; and another at Active Pass, Strait of Georgia, BC, on February 14, 1992. One was at Smithers, BC, on January 9, 1983, for an extremely rare inland record.

Leach's Storm-Petrel
Oceanodroma leucorhoa

Leach's Storm-Petrel is present off the coast in winter, but its status is not well known. It is occasional off southern Vancouver Island in winter. Wahl et al. (1993) consider the species rare off British Columbia and Washington. One bird was seen over the north spit at Coos Bay, OR, during a storm on the 1974 CBC. It is common in offshore Oregon at least into mid-November, as birds have been blown ashore in numbers at that time.

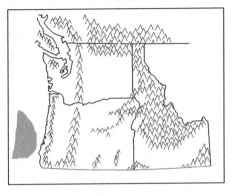

Order PELECANIFORMES
Family Pelecanidae

American White Pelican
Pelecanus erythrorhynchos

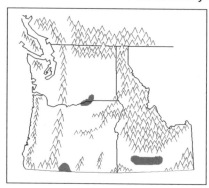

This species is rare in winter in the Klamath Basin and Malheur NWR, OR, and in southern Idaho when water remains open. It is uncommon and local in southeastern Washington and nearly annual in the Lower Columbia Basin since 1983. These birds are very rare north to south-central British Columbia when open water permits. They are rare west of the Cascades, but single birds spent the late winter of 1997 in the Ridgefield-Sauvie Island area near Vancouver, WA, and at Fern Ridge Dam near Eugene, OR.

Brown Pelican
Pelecanus occidentalis

Although most birds leave the Northwest by late November, a few sometimes remain on the outer coast, especially in southern Oregon. In the late 1980s this species remained in numbers at Coos Bay, OR, with the fifty-four birds on the 1987 CBC the state record. In the 1990s this species has become quite rare, with single birds the norm. It is not present at most locations in most years, although a few winter locally each year in Puget Sound. The species has been found at Ocean Shores, WA, and is rare off southern Vancouver Island, BC.

Family Phalacrocoracidae

Double-crested Cormorant
Phalacrocorax auritus

This species is common to locally abundant on the coast in winter, except on the west coast of Vancouver Island, where it is uncommon. Numbers in the protected waters of southern British Columbia have increased greatly since the late 1950s, with a threefold increase in some areas based on CBC data. Though this species has increased at only a 1.4 percent rate in Oregon, it is noticeably more common in winter in the western interior valleys than it was twenty years ago.

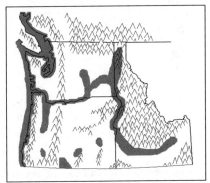

This cormorant is uncommon to occasional inland, mainly along larger rivers and lakes. It is common to abundant along most of the Columbia River east to southeastern Washington, and common to occasional farther east and along the Snake River to southwestern Idaho. Wintering populations inland have generally been increasing, though it is very rare in southern interior British Columbia.

Coastal populations use every water habitat available, from open ocean to estuaries and freshwater lakes. Birds occur upstream to the limit of usable water for fishing, unlike the other two species of cormorant found in the region in winter.

Location	Trend	Circles	Birds/100 ph
BC	3.0	26	10.28
WA	10.4	29	8.93
OR	1.9	24	3.76
ALL	7.3	790	11.96

Brandt's Cormorant
Phalacrocorax penicillatus

Although this species breeds along the Northwest coast, many birds leave the Oregon and Washington outer coast in winter, and it becomes the least common cormorant there in most years. However, it is common to abundant off southern British Columbia, with thousands of birds on CBCs in some years, and occurs in Puget Sound with the greatest abundance along the straits. CBC trends in these areas show a significant increase.

Numbers vary widely from year to year at more southerly sites. Although there are birds all along the Washington and Oregon coasts and concentrations occur, they can be hard to find in some years and sometimes seem rare or absent.

This species does not normally use freshwater habitats and rarely goes very far from the open coast and lower estuaries.

Location	Trend	Circles	Birds/100 ph
BC	18.6	24	49.43
WA	14.0	19	31.85
ALL	3.0	91	46.39

Pelagic Cormorant
Phalacrocorax pelagicus

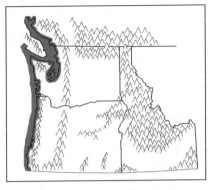

The Pelagic Cormorant is common to abundant along the coast, remaining mainly close to salt water. It is common in Puget Sound and is especially abundant in the Strait of Georgia. CBC trends show a significant increase in Washington waters. In some coastal areas (especially along rocky outer coasts) this is the most common cormorant in winter. It does not normally use freshwater habitats, remaining in the ocean and lower estuaries.

Location	Trend	Circles	Birds/100 ph
BC	-1.5	26	55.07
WA	10.0	23	8.06
ALL	-1.7	98	25.80

Family Fregatidae

Magnificent Frigatebird
Fregata magnificens

This bird is a vagrant from subtropical waters to offshore Oregon and Washington. One was collected on February 18, 1935, at Tillamook Lighthouse, Tillamook County, OR. The unsexed skeleton is specimen number USNM 322266 at the United States National Museum. The skin (which appears to be that of an immature) is museum number 19530 at the San Diego Natural History Museum. Another immature was at Cape Arago, Coos County, OR, on February 1, 1992.

Order CICONIIFORMES
Family Ardeidae

American Bittern
Botaurus lentiginosus

The American Bittern is occasional and widespread in winter in the Fraser lowlands of British Columbia and in the lowlands of western Oregon and Washington, but it can be completely absent where large marshes are not available, e.g. along northern Puget Sound. It is occasional and local east of the Cascades, mainly at large marshes and along major waterways where dense emergent vegetation is available. West of the mountains CBCs with adequate habitat report this species every two to four years, usually single birds.

East of the Cascades in Oregon it is annual at Summer Lake and rare at Malheur NWR and on the Klamath Falls CBC, but the larger Klamath Lake marshes are not widely covered in winter and the species is probably present in small numbers. It is occasional at Tri-Cities, WA, CBC and elsewhere in the Columbia-Snake lowlands. It is absent from Idaho and inland British Columbia in winter. It favors marshes of cattail and bulrush, but also uses areas of dense emergent or seasonally flooded willow (*Salix* spp.).

Location	Trend	Circles	Birds/100 ph
OR	0.3	16	0.14
ALL	-0.9	487	0.12

Great Blue Heron
Ardea herodias

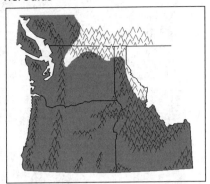

The Great Blue Heron is common to uncommon along almost any open water west of the Cascades, and common to occasional east of the Cascades depending on the availability of open water. West of the Cascades this species can be very common at major estuaries, along slow-moving rivers, and at lakes and ponds. At some locations along the lower Columbia River it can be abundant.

Most birds east of the mountains are along the Columbia-Snake system and major tributaries and in the Klamath Basin. Dozens of birds may concentrate where access to food is possible, often feeding on rodents in dry or frozen areas, and CBCs along the major river systems (such as Tri-Cities, WA, or Klamath Falls, OR) often find thirty or more birds. Smaller numbers winter as far east as northeastern Idaho, mainly along the Snake River and its major tributaries, and north along unfrozen rivers and lakes in southern British Columbia.

Great Egret
Ardea alba

This species breeds in southeastern Oregon, locally in east-central Washington and southern Idaho, and occasionally on the southern Oregon coast. Many birds that breed in California (and perhaps some from inland sources) move north on the coast and inland after the breeding season, and out of this mixture some birds—it is not always clear from which sources—remain to winter.

Great Blue Heron

The bulk of wintering birds in the region are on the southern Oregon coast and in the Klamath Basin. In these areas the species is sometimes common in winter.

On the Oregon coast egrets are common to uncommon north to Coos Bay, where several dozen normally winter. Concentrations of scores of birds are regular in the Coquille Valley when it is flooded. A few birds can be found every year at the Umpqua and Siuslaw estuaries, but north of Florence the species becomes less consistent, with a few birds most years at estuaries such as Yaquina Bay and Tillamook, a few around the mouth of the Columbia River, and very few on the Washington coast. It generally does not occur in Puget Sound in winter and is very rare in British Columbia, where there are about fifteen winter records.

In the western interior valleys of Oregon the pattern is similar. Some birds can generally be found in the Rogue and Umpqua valleys where limited habitat permits. In some years several dozen birds winter at Fern Ridge Reservoir near Eugene, but in most years only half a dozen or so are found on the CBC. Farther north in the Willamette Valley the species is much less common, with single birds here and there north to the Columbia River, where a few are present each year in the Sauvie Island-Ridgefield NWR complex.

Location	Trend	Circles	Birds/100 ph
OR	1.3	21	0.63
ALL	1.7	515	3.52

East of the Cascades, the Great Egret is usually absent, although it has wintered as far east as southwestern Idaho and along the Columbia River in mild years. It is often common in the Klamath Basin during mild winters, but rare in severe winters. It does not normally winter at Summer Lake or Malheur NWR.

The winter of 1995-96 brought the largest number of Great Egrets on record to the region. Over two hundred birds were in the lower Coquille Valley, OR, and at least seventy were in the Sauvie Island-Ridgefield NWR complex west of Vancouver, WA, in early December. Both of these counts were three times normal highs. Outliers from this movement were found elsewhere in the region.

Snowy Egret
Egretta thula

This bird winters only on the southern Oregon coast, where it was first reported in the late 1970s. From 1978 to date, a few birds have wintered almost every year at Coos Bay, with up to eleven birds present in peak years. During this time birds have also been seen in winter at Bandon, Coquille, Reedsport (regularly in the 1980s), and Florence. One bird appeared near Toledo on upper Yaquina Bay in fall 1995.

This expansion of winter range may be due in part to successful breeding on the northern California coast in the past twenty years. The species has not expanded beyond this wintering region to date, and numbers have fluctuated in the early 1990s.

The species has not occurred in Washington, Idaho, or British Columbia in winter.

Little Blue Heron
Egretta caerulea

This bird is a vagrant at any season. The region's first winter record was at Judson Lake on the Whatcom County, Washington-British Columbia border from October 1974 through January 1975 (Weber and Hunn 1978). Another was at Brownsmead, Clatsop County, OR, from January 20 to March 11, 1990.

Cattle Egret
Bubulcus ibis

The Cattle Egret is a rare breeder in southeastern Oregon and southern Idaho. These birds are thought to leave in winter, while birds thought to be from colonies in California move up the west coast in November and December. Some of these remain through the winter, but most disappear. The CBC trend data show a long-term increase, but numbers vary widely from year to year.

Although there are many records of flocks of five to ten birds on the Oregon coast, single birds and smaller groups are the norm. A few reach the coasts of Washington and British Columbia (including Puget Sound and mainland British Columbia) in most years, and some appear in the western interior valleys of Oregon and Washington. The species is very rare in Idaho (December 4, 1980, at Arco [*American Birds* 35: 319]; December 7, 1992, at Lewiston; December 16, 1995, at Hagerman Valley [CBC]), interior British Columbia, eastern Oregon (December 7, 1989, at Galena, Grant County; six birds on December 2, 1986, at Milton-Freewater) and southeastern Washington in early winter.

Green Heron
Butorides virescens

The Green Heron breeds west of the Cascades and very locally on the east side. Many of these birds withdraw in winter, leaving southwestern Oregon the only area where multiple birds are often reported in winter. It is uncommon in the Rogue Valley and on the south coast, occasional farther north in Oregon.

Single birds are reported most winters north to the southern end of Puget Sound; the species is progressively rarer north to southwestern British Columbia, where winter records are few. It is very rare east of the Cascades in winter and a wanderer to southern Idaho, but winterers have been reported from Boise and Pocatello.

Black-crowned Night-Heron
Nycticorax nycticorax

This bird winters by the hundreds in the southern Klamath Basin, and in smaller numbers locally throughout the region. It forms roosts at favored locales, mainly near sizable waterways.

In Oregon, west of the Cascades, this species is

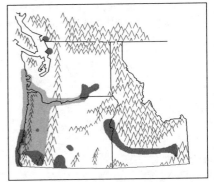

uncommon but visible in the Rogue Valley and more local farther north. The nocturnal habits of these birds combined with their tendency to roost makes them hard to find unless the roost is located. Roosts are known from several sites in western Oregon. Although the species is less common in western Washington it is reported occasionally on the Grays Harbor and Olympia CBCs. It is much rarer farther north. It is rare and local in southwestern British Columbia; the only regular site is Reifel Refuge. It is a vagrant in interior British Columbia and Vancouver Island.

Location	Trend	Circles	Birds/100 ph
OR	-4.8	15	8.41
ALL	2.2	569	1.67

The species' roosting habits affect CBC trend data; the discovery of a roost (or its relocation where observers do not find it) can cause significant swings in the number of birds reported.

East of the mountains the major roosts are at Klamath Falls, OR, where several hundred birds winter. Smaller numbers are reported from Summer Lake, OR, the Tri-Cities area, WA, and other sites, mainly along the Columbia-Snake system to southern Idaho and at major marshes.

Family Threskiornithidae

White-faced Ibis
Plegadis chihi

There are very few winter records in the region for this bird. The only winter record for British Columbia is of one bird in winter 1986-87 at Hardy Bay on Vancouver Island. One was at Tillamook, OR, on December 15, 1979 (Gilligan et al. 1994). Four ibis presumably of this species were on the Sauvie Island, OR, CBC in 1981.

Family Cathartidae

Turkey Vulture
Cathartes aura

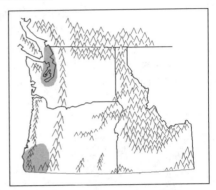

The Turkey Vulture is rare but regular in winter west of the Cascades, with most reports coming from southwestern Oregon and the Puget Sound-southwest British Columbia area. It lingers more often in the latter area than in southwestern Washington or northwestern Oregon, and is most regular in Oregon in the Rogue River counties. It is occasional in winter to interior British Columbia, and rare in southeastern Washington. There is at least one winter record from central Oregon.

Some spring migrants are found in most years by late February in western Oregon and sometimes to Washington.

Order ANSERIFORMES
Family Anatidae
Subfamily Anserinae

Fulvous Whistling-Duck
Dendrocygna bicolor

Eleven birds were found at Horsfall Lake, Coos County, OR, February 14-24, 1970. One bird was collected and photos were taken (Schmidt 1988). These may not have been of wild origin.

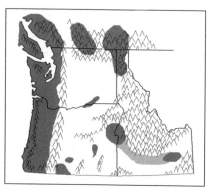

Tundra Swan
Cygnus columbianus

The Tundra Swan winters locally in large numbers west of the Cascades and in smaller numbers in the lakes of south-central Oregon and southern Idaho. It is local in small numbers in eastern Washington, at lakes and rivers in southern British Columbia and in the Idaho panhandle, and elsewhere east of the Cascades.

This species concentrates at favored areas each year, including the Willamette Valley, northern Puget Sound, Summer Lake, OR, Klamath Lake, OR, American Falls Reservoir, ID, the Okanagan Valley, the Columbia River valley west of the gorge, and at coastal locations, especially in Oregon. It is an occasional migrant into early December in the Salmon River region of east-central Idaho (Roberts 1992).

Numbers range from up to a thousand or more at Summer and Klamath lakes to scattered birds at small estuaries. Numbers vary considerably from year to year. CBC trend data suggest that long-term increases in wintering birds are more significant in the southern parts of the region.

Location	Trend	Circles	Birds/100 ph
BC	0.0	23	2.35
WA	3.3	19	3.30
OR	5.8	35	42.42
ALL	3.4	683	14.74

Bewick's Swan (*C.c. bewickii*) has been found in the region in winter. One was at Sauvie Island, Multnomah County, OR, on January 2, 1982. Bewick's Swan was lumped with Whistling Swan in the 6th Edition of the *AOU Check-list* to form the new species named Tundra Swan.

Whooper Swan
Cygnus cygnus

A bird was at Lower Klamath NWR, OR-CA, from late fall through early winter, 1991. It was seen in Oregon on December 13. This or another bird was seen in late fall of 1993-95 at Summer Lake Wildlife Area in Lake County, OR. In 1994 and 1995 it remained into early December.

Whooper Swan

Summer Lake, OR
(Photograph by
Harry B. Nehls)

Trumpeter Swan
Cygnus buccinator

This species is expanding its numbers and winter range in the region. In the 1960s it was rare away from southwest British Columbia, southeastern Idaho, and northern Puget Sound, except for introduced or local populations. Today it is locally common on some open water in British Columbia and northwestern Washington. It is uncommon south to northwestern Oregon and northern Idaho, with small numbers in southwestern Idaho along the Snake River and on other open water.

East of the Cascades it is regular in British Columbia, northeastern Idaho and at introduction sites at Malheur NWR and Summer Lake, OR. Recently, small numbers have been found regularly in southern Idaho. Marked birds from introduced U.S. populations and from Alaska and Canada have

Location	Trend	Circles	Birds/100 ph
BC	11.8	32	14.43
WA	13.7	16	1.43
ALL	10.4	89	3.92

been seen at many locations throughout the region in recent years. Unmarked birds, presumably migrating into the area from the north, are also being seen more often. Single birds have been found as far from major wintering grounds as Lake Owyhee and Wallowa Lake, OR.

West of the Cascades hundreds of birds can be found regularly in British Columbia and northwestern Washington, with the greatest concentrations on Vancouver Island and in the Fraser lowlands. The center of winter abundance is at Comox, Vancouver Island, with up to fourteen hundred birds. Hundreds of birds can be found in northwestern Washington where the species was essentially absent before 1970. Jewett et al. (1953) note that the species "doubtless occurred in large numbers in earlier days" in Washington, based on a variety of reports and specimens. Today the mean Bellingham, WA, CBC tally is 101.9 and the high is 297 (Wahl 1995).

Several dozen birds have been present each winter in northwestern Oregon (mostly on the north coast and in the northern Willamette Valley) since the late 1980s. The lower Columbia River and adjacent waterways of Oregon and Washington have become regular wintering grounds for small numbers of this species. Only the southwestern corner of Oregon is now outside the annual occurrence of the species in this region.

Mute Swan
Cygnus olor

This bird has been introduced locally in the region. About two hundred birds are now self-sustaining on southern Vancouver Island and a small population in King County, WA, is considered to be self-sustaining. The population at Bend, OR, may also be self-sustaining.

Greater White-fronted Goose
Anser albifrons

Hundreds of these geese normally winter in the Klamath Basin, and numbers begin to build up at Summer Lake, OR, from mid- to late February. Small numbers, often just one or two birds, can be found in most years scattered over western Oregon (and occasionally in Washington) where other waterfowl gather. They are 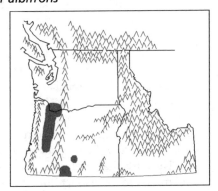 less regular in British Columbia but small numbers are usually present in the southwestern part of the province. They are rare in winter in the Okanagan Valley of British Columbia, eastern Washington, and Idaho, although some northbound migrants may begin coming through in late February.

Location	Trend	Circles	Birds/100 ph
BC	0.3	19	0.18
OR	-0.7	24	1.06
WA	0.5	16	0.05
ALL	7.5	389	15.97

Snow Goose
Chen caerulescens

The Snow Goose is locally abundant in southwestern British Columbia (Fraser lowlands) and on the Skagit delta, WA. It is common to uncommon but local elsewhere in northern Puget Sound and in the Klamath Basin of Oregon-California. It is regular in small numbers in south-central Oregon (Lake County) and in the Sauvie Island, OR-Ridgefield NWR,

Location	Trend	Circles	Birds/100 ph
BC	24.6	15	23.12
WA	-7.2	17	148.28
OR	12.5	26	1.32
ALL	-2.3	967	85.59

WA, area. It is occasional to rare in southern Idaho and interior British Columbia and Washington, except that some birds use the Columbia River bottomlands in most years. It is a rare straggler through December in eastern Idaho. Snow Geese are sometimes found with large flocks of Canada Geese.

The birds that winter in the Fraser lowlands follow a migration route distinct from those that use the Klamath Basin, even though many birds in both areas originate on Wrangel Island, Russia. Fraser birds come down the coast while Klamath birds use an inland route. Marked birds use the same wintering grounds from year to year with very little crossover. See the excellent discussion in Campbell et al. (1990) for details. See also Gilligan et al. (1994) for a discussion of the routes and origin of Oregon winter birds.

Ross' Goose
Chen rossii

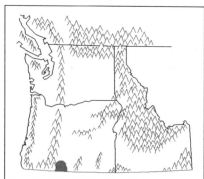

This goose is common in most years in the Klamath Basin, otherwise rare in the region in winter. Most birds winter in the Central Valley of California, with some in the southwest. Because of this species' migration path from north-central Canada to California by way of southern Idaho and southeastern Oregon (where it moves through in late February), it is a vagrant in western British Columbia (there are about seven records in the Vancouver area), Washington, and northern Idaho and a rare wanderer to western Oregon. It is rare but regular in eastern Washington and very rare in southern Idaho in winter.

Emperor Goose
Chen canagica

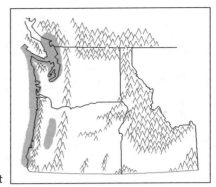

The Emperor Goose is rare but regular on the coast and an extremely rare visitor to coastal southwestern British Columbia. It is rare in the Willamette Valley and the Klamath Basin. There have been a few inland reports elsewhere in the region except in Idaho, which has not recorded the species at any season.

Coastal birds are typically alone or in very small flocks; inland birds are typically found with Canada Geese or other waterfowl. This arctic breeder winters mainly in western Alaska and the Aleutians, but a few birds are present in the region every year.

Emperor Geese

*Netarts Bay, OR
(Photograph by Skip
Russell)*

Brant
Branta bernicla

The Brant is common but highly local along the coast. The most regular concentration points are at Yaquina Bay and Tillamook Bay, OR, in central Puget Sound, WA, and Boundary Bay, BC. It was formerly common in winter at Coos Bay, OR, but is now occasional, possibly because of a reduction in available eelgrass, the principal food source.

Populations along the southern British Columbia coast have dropped drastically, with the greatest reduction occurring from the late 1950s through the late 1960s. Winter populations have never again approached earlier numbers, but have increased again recently to over two hundred at Boundary Bay. It is rarely reported inland at any season, but is occasional in the Willamette Valley, and has occurred in central Oregon and Idaho. Most inland records are with Canada Geese.

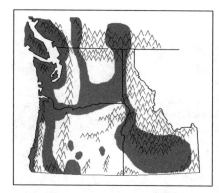

Canada Goose
Branta canadensis

This species is uncommon to locally abundant and is found throughout the region. Principal wintering grounds include the Klamath Basin, Willamette Valley, lower Columbia basin of Washington and adjacent Oregon, the lakes of south-central Oregon, the lakes of northern Idaho, and the Snake River valley and nearby lakes.

Several populations winter in the region and use distinctly different areas. Fuller discussions of these populations can be found in state and provincial studies, in Bellrose (1976), and (in summary form) in Madge and Burn (1988).

Location	Trend	Circles	Birds/100 ph
BC	8.6	42	53.97
ID	-0.7	17	331.08
WA	5.8	31	52.31
OR	3.2	42	165.70
ALL	1.7	1662	289.31

Subfamily Anatinae

Wood Duck
Aix sponsa

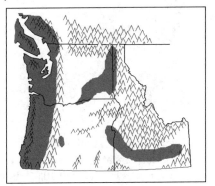

This species winters mainly west of the Cascades from southwestern British Columbia southward, though it is less common in winter than in summer; many birds leave the region in winter. It is most common in southwestern Oregon and locally common to occasional east of the Cascades at lowland locations where open water is available, especially in the Snake River valley of southeastern Washington to southern Idaho. It is rare in winter east of the Cascades in British Columbia, northern Washington, and montane Idaho.

CBC trend data show a slight increase regionwide with more birds staying in colder parts of the region than previously known. Although some field guides and other references show the species as absent in winter from the Snake River valley of southern Idaho and the adjacent lower Owyhee valley of Oregon, it does winter locally there.

Location	Trend	Circles	Birds/100 ph
BC	4.6	19	1.03
WA	3.3	23	0.24
OR	6.2	27	0.86
ALL	0.5	1247	1.77

Green-winged Teal
Anas crecca

This is one of the most common and hardy ducks that winters in the region. It is locally abundant west of the Cascades (especially in Oregon and along Puget Sound) and common almost anywhere there is open still or slow-moving water. East of the mountains it remains to winter in most of the region where open water is available, and is quite common in some areas such as the Columbia lowlands of southeastern

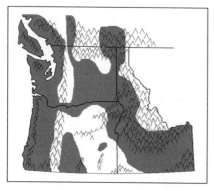

Washington and nearby Oregon, the southern Oregon lake basins, and the Snake River valley of Idaho. Some birds remain north to northern and northeastern Idaho and eastern British Columbia when open water permits; in some years this species is frozen out of the northeastern part of the region, as it prefers shallower water than most other ducks that winter in the region.

Numbers at preferred sites can reach the thousands, with CBC peaks in excess of 10,000 birds in some years. Trend data show that the species is becoming more common in the northern and inland parts of the region.

Location	Trend	Circles	Birds/100 ph
BC	4.9	38	16.99
ID	1.4	16	12.32
WA	3.5	33	19.13
OR	0.4	43	12.85
ALL	1.3	1304	28.46

Baikal Teal
Anas formosa

A male was collected by a hunter at Irish Bend, Benton County, OR on January 12, 1974. The specimen is in the Oregon State University Collection.

Falcated Duck
Anas falcata

This species is a vagrant. An adult male was shot by a hunter at Naselle River, Pacific County, WA, on January 3, 1979. The mounted specimen is in possession of the hunter. One was at Tofino, Vancouver Island, January 20-April 1995.

American Black Duck
Anas rubripes

This bird is rare and has not been reported as often in the past twenty years, perhaps as a consequence of declining eastern populations and interbreeding with Mallards. The presence of small but successful introduced populations in southwestern British Columbia and near Everett, WA, clouds the origin of modern records of the species in the region.

Oregon has five specimen records of this species. Two were obtained in January and March 1950 near Ontario (Gilligan et al., 1994). The state's most recent specimen record was from Malheur NWR in 1977.

Idaho's only winter record was February 7, 1980, near Pocatello (*American Birds* 34(3): 292).

Mallard
Anas platyrhynchos

This is the most widespread, hardy, and in some areas abundant wintering duck in the region. Thousands of birds winter at some sites such as the Fraser delta in British Columbia, the grain country of south-central Washington, and Lake Lowell in southwestern Idaho. The major wintering population at Lake Lowell is no doubt one 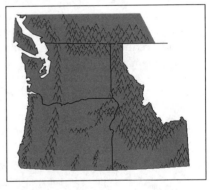 reason for the high birds per party hour ratio in Idaho. The Klamath basin also supports large wintering flocks. Anywhere that open water is available, this adaptable duck will winter; it is least abundant in southwestern Oregon. Some groups of males winter together.

Location	Trend	Circles	Birds/100 ph
BC	3.3	47	77.94
ID	-12.6	18	4362.69
WA	-0.2	36	156.87
OR	2.2	45	148.45
ALL	-6.7	1928	597.67

Northern Pintail
Anas acuta

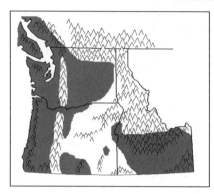

The Northern Pintail winters throughout the region where open water is available, with most birds concentrating in the lake basins, estuaries, and refuges with other waterfowl. It is locally abundant but often one of the least common dabbling ducks present. It generally does not remain in numbers in colder areas. It is rare and local in northern Idaho and generally absent from eastern British Columbia and northeastern Washington by mid-winter (except on major waterways and lakes), although lingerers sometimes remain into December.

This species has suffered periods of decline nationally but Northwest trends are mixed, with a clear drop in Idaho and some reduction in Oregon, while numbers in British Columbia have remained steady and Washington data show an increase.

Location	Trend	Circles	Birds/100 ph
BC	0.8	38	50.01
ID	-19.5	15	91.11
WA	3.9	32	35.16
OR	-5.1	39	62.86
ALL	-5.2	1342	134.02

Blue-winged Teal
Anas discors

This bird is rare in winter, with most records coming from coastal sites and the western interior valleys. A few are reported in most years in western Oregon and Washington. It is rare in winter in southwestern British Columbia, very rare in the Okanagan Valley, eastern Washington, and central Oregon. There are no winter records known for Idaho or far-eastern Oregon.

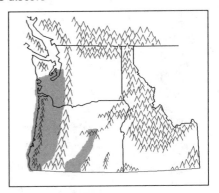

Cinnamon Teal
Anas cyanoptera

The Cinnamon Teal is rare but annual in winter west of the Cascades, very rare east of the Cascades. It is locally annual or nearly so, even in numbers up to ten or twenty birds, at a very few preferred sites. Astoria, Eugene, and Medford, OR, occasionally report this species wintering in small flocks. Most northern Oregon and Puget Sound sites report the species somewhat less often, and it is very rare in the Klamath Basin. There are a few instances of birds remaining into early winter in eastern Oregon and Idaho, but the species is not known to overwinter there or in the northeastern part of the region. It is very rare north to the Okanagan Valley, BC, in early winter.

Northern Shoveler
Anas clypeata

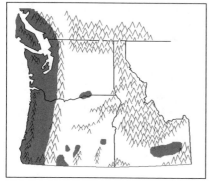

This bird is common west of the Cascades in shallow water and locally abundant from western Oregon north to Puget Sound, less common farther north. East of the mountains it is less common but present when open water is available north to southern Idaho, southern Washington, and British Columbia. In eastern Oregon, it is abundant at Lake Abert but less common elsewhere. It is rare after December in British Columbia, northern Idaho, and northeastern Washington. The northern edge of winter range where it is present annually in numbers east of the Cascades is southeastern Washington, where it is common in most years along the Columbia River and its tributaries and at other sites with open water. It is rare (absent most years) at Yakima, Ellensburg, Spokane, and other northerly sites.

CBC trend data show a slight decrease in the region.

Location	Trend	Circles	Birds/100 ph
BC	-2.7	28	1.74
WA	-2.2	32	4.49
OR	-3.9	32	11.04
ALL	3.3	1020	21.19

Gadwall
Anas strepera

This hardy duck is present throughout the region in winter in a variety of habitats where open water is available. It winters in small numbers in most of the region, but these numbers may be increasing based on CBC trend data, especially in Washington.

It is abundant to uncommon west of the Cascades throughout the region. It is locally common east of the Cascades north to southeastern Washington, and present north to south-central British Columbia in small numbers, including the region east of the Cascades. It is uncommon in southern Idaho, occasional at lakes in the panhandle.

Numbers can exceed a thousand on occasion at preferred sites, but a few dozen to a few hundred is the norm. This species appears to prefer certain sites and to concentrate there; examples include the Tri-Cities area of southeastern Washington, Coos Bay and Summer Lake, OR, and the Klamath Basin.

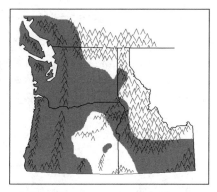

Location	Trend	Circles	Birds/100 ph
BC	5.8	28	2.69
WA	17.3	32	5.12
OR	2.9	35	11.62
ALL	3.2	1238	13.64

Eurasian Wigeon
Anas penelope

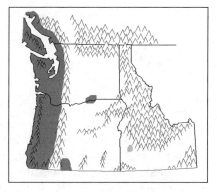

The Eurasian Wigeon is uncommon to occasional west of the Cascades; two or three birds can often be found in large flocks of American Wigeon, but larger concentrations are rare. Nonetheless, CBCs have found over a dozen birds on many occasions, and a flock of twenty males was at Roberts Bank, BC, on January 3, 1994. It is most common in northwestern Washington, where the Skagit Flats harbor many birds.

Location	Trend	Circles	Birds/100 ph
BC	2.9	20	0.17
WA	2.0	28	0.22
OR	3.0	19	0.10
ALL	2.7	218	0.07

East of the Cascades this is a much rarer bird, absent most years at most sites. Three to five males are now found annually in southeast Washington (M. Denny, personal communication) and they are almost annual in recent winters in Idaho. The region shows a slight increase over time which is echoed by more reports of the species from the eastern part of the region.

American Wigeon
Anas americana

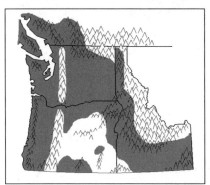

The American Wigeon is common to abundant west of the Cascades, where it can be found in flocks of thousands at large estuaries and lakes. This species is usually more common than Mallard or Northern Pintail along the coast of Oregon and Washington. It is often the most common wintering duck in the western interior valleys of Oregon, and is often more common than Mallard and Pintail in the Puget Sound area. This predominance does not extend to the northern sound or British Columbia, where Mallards and Pintail are more common except at some coastal wetlands.

East of the Cascades this species is abundant to occasional depending on the availability of open water. Few birds winter north of central Washington except along major rivers and lakes. It is regular in numbers up to the low hundreds north to the Okanagan Valley. Numbers in the lake basins of southeastern Oregon range from a handful to the high hundreds.

CBC data show a slight decrease over time throughout the region.

Location	Trend	Circles	Birds/100 ph
BC	-0.4	37	99.43
WA	-1.5	36	120.42
OR	-3.4	40	86.39
ALL	-1.2	1307	88.36

Canvasback
Aythya valisineria

This bird is abundant to uncommon west of the Cascades, with major concentrations at coastal estuaries and larger rivers and lakes. Hundreds can be found at some sites, such as the estuary of the Columbia River.

It is widespread but usually in small numbers east of the Cascades, and absent at some locations in some years. It concentrates on the Columbia River near grain elevators. It is occasional to northeastern Washington and lakes in the Idaho panhandle. Numbers east of the Cascades increase when lakes begin to thaw in late February, but this species is not common anywhere east of the mountains except on the largest waterways: in the Klamath Basin, along the Columbia River, and locally north to Okanagan Lake and vicinity. It is occasional to uncommon along the Snake River and major lakes of southern Idaho, but is progressively rarer farther east and does not always overwinter.

Location	Trend	Circles	Birds/100 ph
WA	-0.8	33	5.04
OR	-2.8	30	9.81
BC	0.3	31	2.22
ALL	-1.0	1211	12.93

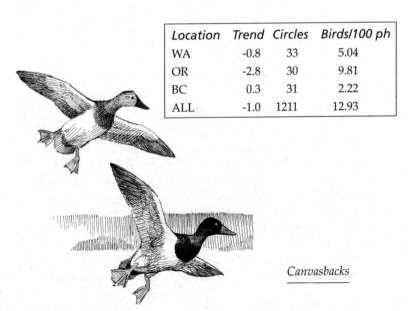

Canvasbacks

43

Redhead
Aythya americana

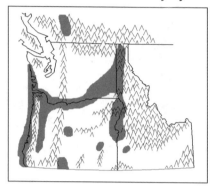

This species is among the most highly local of wintering birds. Hundreds may use one site while nearby areas that appear equally suitable to a human eye never see the species.

Redheads winter in small numbers throughout the region where open water is available, but are absent from many areas. The principal concentration points are Okanagan Lake, southeastern Washington, and the Columbia River (especially near grain elevators), southern Idaho (with some in the panhandle), and Coos Bay, OR. Most birds are at these locations.

Redheads are rare to occasional in the western interior valleys of Oregon and occasional to uncommon along most of the Oregon coast. They are occasional to uncommon in the Puget Sound area and southwestern British Columbia.

Location	Trend	Circles	Birds/100 ph
BC	-4.9	20	12.89
WA	6.8	24	3.42
OR	-1.3	23	3.34
ALL	-3.4	1125	53.56

Ring-necked Duck
Aythya collaris

This species winters locally throughout the region where open water is available. It generally avoids deep salt water and is therefore not often found in lower estuaries. It is most abundant at ponds, lakes, and backwaters west of the Cascades, where hundreds can sometimes be found in preferred habitat and small flocks of a few to a dozen or more can be found on most freshwater lakes.

East of the Cascades the species can be found in similar habitat, and is uncommon to locally abundant north to lakes and major rivers in eastern Washington and the Idaho panhandle, where hundreds can be found locally. It is less common but present every year north to the Okanagan Valley and other sites in southern British Columbia where open water is available, and in southern Idaho in similar locales. At major lakes it can be locally abundant.

CBC data show a slight increase in Oregon and a significant increase in Washington over time, while British Columbia numbers have been essentially stable.

Location	Trend	Circles	Birds/100 ph
BC	0.5	32	3.07
WA	8.6	34	12.59
OR	2.8	35	8.12
ALL	-1.1	1336	10.74

Tufted Duck
Aythya fuligula

This species is a rare vagrant to western British Columbia and the Okanagan Valley, Washington, and Oregon; it is of nearly annual occurrence. There is a generally accepted record from Wenatchee, WA, on January 17-19 and February 17, 1986 (*American Birds* 40: 305). It has not been recorded east of the Cascades or from Idaho in winter, although there was a bird at Antelope Reservoir, Malheur County, OR, in November, 1995. It is most often reported with flocks of Ring-necked Ducks at small ponds.

Greater Scaup
Aythya marila

The Greater Scaup is uncommon to abundant in estuaries and on major rivers near the coast throughout the region. Huge rafts of this species, often mixed with Lesser Scaup, can be found at some locations, while nearby only a few birds or none can be

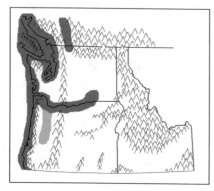

found. It is generally absent from the open ocean and from smaller rivers and ponds, but uses large lakes near the coast.

Away from the coast this species is found mainly along the Columbia River (especially near grain terminals) and at the largest lakes, although it is uncommon to occasional throughout the region west of the Cascades. East of the mountains it is occasional on open water east to Idaho, where it is rare in winter (occasional at the largest lakes). It is, however, uncommon to common along the Columbia River to east-central Washington, and it is the predominant winter scaup in the Okanagan region of British Columbia, where it is locally abundant.

Confusion about the identification of the two scaup has clouded winter records in the region, although CBC data show a slight decrease except in Oregon. It is quite clear that the species is much more common than once believed, especially on major inland bodies of water and east of the Cascades. It can be expected in winter throughout the region where deep open water permits.

Location	Trend	Circles	Birds/100 ph
BC	-4.4	37	34.03
WA	-7.4	30	15.18
OR	5.6	21	6.39
ALL	-3.4	807	7.83

Lesser Scaup
Aythya affinis

The Lesser Scaup winters throughout the region where deep open water is available. It is most abundant at estuaries (where it prefers up-river areas), coastal rivers, the Columbia-Snake system (especially near grain terminals), and major inland lakes.

See Greater Scaup (above) for a discussion of uncertainties about distribution. Although this species was once considered "the" inland scaup in the region, it is clear that in some areas away from the ocean the Greater Scaup is as regular and sometimes more common.

Numbers in the thousands can be found at favored wintering grounds. CBC data show a significant decrease in Idaho and mixed trends elsewhere in the region.

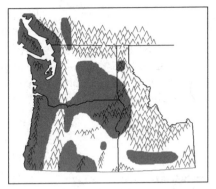

Location	Trend	Circles	Birds/100 ph
BC	2.2	32	4.91
ID	-8.7	14	63.56
WA	-1.3	32	18.70
OR	5.0	36	11.36
ALL	-1.6	1427	19.78

Common Eider
Somateria mollissima

This species is a possible vagrant to the region in winter. Jewett et al. (1953) note that "Bowles saw a flock of seven individuals and later two others, females, on the Nisqually flats, January 6, 1906." However, the Washington Bird Records Committee has unanimously rejected this report (Mattocks and Aanerud 1997). Jewett et al. also mention that the same observer saw a male in the same general area from a ship a few days later and that Dawson listed the species for south Puget Sound on February 9, 1906, perhaps referring to the same birds. No further information is available regarding these records. There are no accepted records for Washington.

Earl Larrison and others observed a pair on Mann Lake near Lewiston, ID, on April 16, 1977, the only record for Idaho (Taylor and Trost 1987). However, this record is viewed with skepticism by some Idaho observers. The only British Columbia records are two in the northern part of the province in late fall. The species has not been documented elsewhere in the region.

King Eider
Somateria spectabilis

This species is a vagrant to British Columbia and southward along the coast. There are about eight winter records in the portion of British Columbia covered in this book and eight in Washington. There are about seven winter records in Oregon.

Steller's Eider
Polysticta stelleri

Steller's Eider
———————
Coos Bay, OR
(Photograph by
Harry B. Nehls)

This is a vagrant to the region. A female was at Sidney, BC, from February 13 through March 1976. An adult male was at Port Townsend, Jefferson County, WA, from October 18, 1986 to February 8, 1987. An adult male was at the north jetty of Coos Bay, Coos County, OR, February 10-18, 1992.

Harlequin Duck
Histrionicus histrionicus

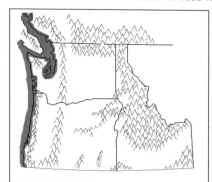

The Harlequin Duck is common to uncommon along rocky shores, jetties, and similar rough-water situations along the region's coast in winter. It is regular in British Columbia and in Puget Sound (locally common) south to Seattle; numbers dwindle south to Olympia, mainly because habitat is more limited. This species is not abundant anywhere in the region, but can be found in small groups all along the coast where habitat permits.

Location	Trend	Circles	Birds/100 ph
BC	-0.9	30	6.03
WA	6.0	18	2.68
ALL	-0.8	199	1.11

Harlequin Ducks

Away from the ocean this species is very rare in winter except in interior British Columbia, where it is occasional. A female was at Walla Walla, WA, from November 1995 to March 1996, and Yakima and Spokane counties in Washington have about three winter records each. There is one inland winter record from Oregon (Rogue River, Jackson County on December 29, 1990), and none from Idaho.

Oldsquaw
Clangula hyemalis

The Oldsquaw is abundant to uncommon along the region's coast, sometimes in the company of scoters. This species favors sheltered waters although it can also be seen on the open ocean. It is locally abundant in the waters of northern Puget Sound and north along the straits into British Columbia, where over a hundred birds can be found on CBCs on occasion. From the Seattle area southward, there are no such major concentration

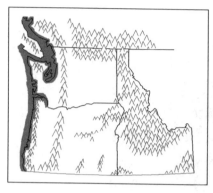

points in the region, with numbers under ten birds the norm, and no birds some years at a given location.

The Oldsquaw is also prone to show up on ponds and lakes far from the ocean, even east of the Cascades where open water is available. It has been found on several occasions in the Okanagan Valley in winter, and there are several early winter records from Idaho and eastern Washington and Oregon.

Location	Trend	Circles	Birds/100 ph
BC	-4.8	26	153.02
WA	5.6	22	3.38
ALL	0.0	661	22.48

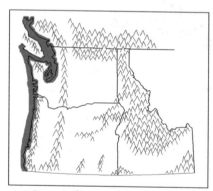

Black Scoter
Melanitta nigra

This is the least common and most local scoter in most of the region, but is widespread along the coast, not straying from the ocean and lower estuaries. This species is much more common in British Columbia and Washington, including Puget Sound, than it is along the Oregon coast. CBC tallies in the scores or hundreds are not uncommon north of the Columbia, especially in Puget Sound and the straits, while the species can be hard to find in Oregon except as a token pair or small flock here and there. It is especially spotty on the central and southern coast. The highest numbers in Oregon are typically in northern Lincoln County and locally in Tillamook and southern Clatsop counties, where this species can sometimes be found in the hundreds.

Location	Trend	Circles	Birds/100 ph
BC	-3.1	25	26.35
WA	4.1	21	6.14
ALL	-3.1	368	5.17

This scoter rarely strays from salt water.

Surf Scoter
Melanitta perspicillata

The Surf Scoter is abundant along the entire coast of the region, forming large flocks at most sites. It is hard to visit the ocean in winter without having some of these birds in sight. This is usually the most common scoter in the region, with flocks in the scores to hundreds of birds not uncommon at favored sites. This species can often be found well up coastal estuaries, and, though it is rare inland, has been recorded inland numerous

Surf Scoters and Oldsquaw

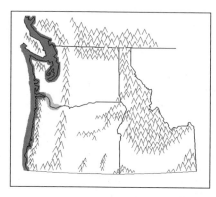

times, mainly west of the Cascades. It has been recorded in winter as a rare wanderer to eastern Oregon and Washington, the Okanagan Valley, and southwestern Idaho.

A regional record 11,528 were found on the 1995 Vancouver, BC, CBC.

Location	Trend	Circles	Birds/100 ph
BC	-2.4	29	33.97
WA	3.1	25	25.36
OR	3.0	17	8.16
ALL	-1.0	395	11.35

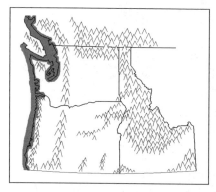

White-winged Scoter
Melanitta fusca

This scoter is abundant to uncommon along the coast, and numbers seem to vary more from year to year at a given site than for the other scoters. For example, CBC counts have ranged from 64 to 916 at Bellingham, WA, and from 37 to 1,622 at Tillamook Bay, OR. These swings do not occur so strongly in either Black or Surf Scoter.

Like the Surf Scoter, this species is rare inland throughout the region, although it may be somewhat more regular than that species as a late-fall migrant or early-winter wanderer in some areas east of the Cascades.

Location	Trend	Circles	Birds/100 ph
BC	-4.0	29	21.71
WA	-1.8	27	24.43
ALL	-1.4	534	4.34

Common Goldeneye
Bucephala clangula

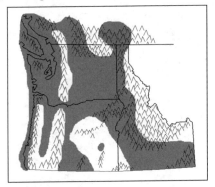

This bird is uncommon to locally abundant throughout the region in winter where open water is available, except on open ocean. This is one of the most common winter diving ducks in much of the region, with concentrations of hundreds of birds at many sites in Puget Sound, in the Klamath Basin, and all along the Columbia-Snake system. These birds are especially widespread and common in southern Idaho. Smaller numbers can be found on almost any sizable patch of open water in the region, especially east of the Cascades. A stunning concentration of about five thousand birds (groups of up to 750 birds together) was present in a 3-mile stretch of the Snake River between Farewell Bend and Annex, Malheur County, OR, on January 8, 1995 (*Oregon Birds* 21(3): 93).

This species uses both fresh and salt water, but generally avoids very small ponds and unsheltered open ocean. It is widespread in the region's estuaries, but usually not in the numbers found east of the Cascades. It is not common on rough water, thus it is often in the upper parts of estuaries rather than by jetties or rocky openings. The Grays Harbor, WA, count averages 26 per year; Tillamook Bay, OR, averages 117; Coos Bay, OR, averages 21.

This species is less common in southwestern Oregon than elsewhere in the region, and is not especially common in the western interior valleys. It is found on about two-thirds of Sauvie Island, OR, CBCs, but on only about half of Salem or Eugene, OR, counts.

Location	Trend	Circles	Birds/100 ph
BC	-2.4	45	17.04
ID	-4.3	16	22.44
WA	0.2	36	14.79
OR	4.0	39	10.11
ALL	-1.1	1607	17.46

Barrow's Goldeneye
Bucephala islandica

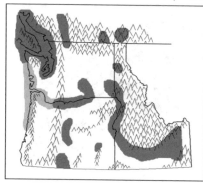

This duck is abundant in parts of the region in winter and completely absent elsewhere. It is most common in the Strait of Georgia, Puget Sound, and locally east of the Cascades.

The center of winter population is along the southern coast of mainland British Columbia and in Puget Sound. The Vancouver, BC, CBC holds the all-time record of 3,388 and other counts have exceeded a thousand birds. Counts in the hundreds on waters off southern mainland British Columbia are regular.

In Washington, Bellingham averages 124 birds on its CBC, Seattle 94, Tacoma 186, and Olympia 523. The contrast between Olympia, with the highest densities in the sound, and Portland and Sauvie Island, OR, a mere 100 miles to the south with plenty of open water, is remarkable: each of the Oregon counts had reported a single bird once in thirty and twenty-two years, respectively. Even on the coast due west of Olympia the species is not found every year at Grays Harbor, and it is rare to occasional in winter along the Oregon coast; it is essentially absent south of Alsea Bay, Lincoln County, in most years. It is rare in the western interior valleys of Oregon and southwestern Washington in winter, but can be found on unfrozen Cascade lakes, sometimes in numbers.

East of the Cascades this species is fairly common, but tends to concentrate at favored locations, leaving few birds elsewhere. Between three and five thousand have been noted at Lewiston, ID, in recent winters, and there were two hundred at Brownlee Dam, Baker County, OR, in January 1980. Numbers in the southern Snake River valley are usually more modest, while it is generally absent from the upper Salmon River valley (Roberts 1992). It winters in the Okanagan Valley, mainly on the Okanagan River, where it is uncommon. Small flocks can also be found on other lakes in southern British Columbia.

Farther south, it is uncommon to common along the Columbia-Snake system. The largest concentrations in eastern

Location	Trend	Circles	Birds/100 ph
BC	2.6	43	8.12
WA	3.1	25	5.59
OR	5.6	16	1.13
ALL	2.1	317	7.10

Oregon are in the Klamath Basin, where an average forty-three birds are found on the Klamath Falls CBC, and along the Columbia and Snake Rivers. In Idaho numbers range up to a few dozen on CBCs with plenty of open water, but the species is sometimes absent. It is much less common—even rare—away from major rivers, and appears to prefer rivers to lakes in winter in parts of the region.

A slight regionwide increase over time is apparent from CBC data.

Bufflehead
Bucephala albeola

The Bufflehead is common to abundant west of the Cascades, uncommon to locally common east of the mountains on open water. Large concentrations of Bufflehead can be found at estuaries, along major rivers and lakes, and in protected areas of Puget Sound and the straits. Flocks can number in the hundreds at preferred sites (locally thousands at, e.g., Coos Bay, OR), and pairs and small flocks can be found even on small lakes, sloughs, and backwaters throughout the region where open water permits. This species generally avoids open ocean.

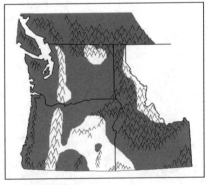

Location	Trend	Circles	Birds/100 ph
BC	-0.4	44	18.50
WA	0.5	35	20.04
OR	2.4	36	15.69
ALL	0.6	1388	8.32

Smew
Mergellus albellus

This is a vagrant to the region from Asia. One was at Reifel refuge in southwest British Columbia in February 1974 and again in January 1975. An adult male was at Langley and Surrey, BC, from December 30, 1989, to February 1, 1990. Some of these records may refer to escaped birds, since the species is regularly kept in captivity in the Vancouver area.

An adult male was at Willard, Skamania County, WA, on December 28, 1989. The following winter, an adult male was near that area in the Columbia River Gorge at Stevenson, Skamania County, WA, and Hood River County, OR, from January 26 to April 1, 1991. Presumably the same bird returned the following winter and remained in the area from January 2 to February 16, 1992, when it vanished after sustaining serious injuries from an unknown source.

Hooded Merganser
Lophodytes cucullatus

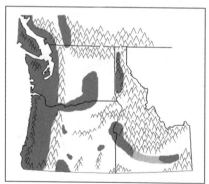

This species is uncommon to common west of the Cascades, uncommon to occasional and local east of the mountains.

Although some field guide maps do not indicate that this species is regular east of the Cascades, it is in fact a common winter bird in the Okanagan Valley, regular in small numbers in the Idaho panhandle and along the Columbia-Snake River system, and uncommon to occasional even to southeastern Idaho. It is also common in winter in the southern part of Malheur NWR and in central Oregon (Bend area). A concentration of forty-five birds along the Snake River at Farewell Bend, Baker-Malheur counties, OR, on December 28, 1994 (John Gatchet, personal communication) is one of the larger flocks found so far east in winter.

West of the mountains this species is most common in western Oregon and southwestern British Columbia (including

Vancouver Island), where numerous small rivers, lakes, and ponds provide considerable habitat. It can be found throughout the region in this kind of location. Like the Common Merganser, this species generally avoids salt water, although it can sometimes be found in lower estuaries.

CBC data show a slight increase regionwide.

Location	Trend	Circles	Birds/100 ph
BC	2.7	38	2.95
WA	6.3	34	2.30
OR	1.5	37	2.02
ALL	5.2	1327	2.43

Common Merganser
Mergus merganser

The Common Merganser is uncommon to abundant and winters throughout the region where open water permits. It prefers larger rivers and lakes, but will use smaller features as well. It often forms large rafts of scores or even hundreds of birds at favored locations (many hundreds on Fern Ridge Reservoir, Lane County, OR; up to 3,000 on

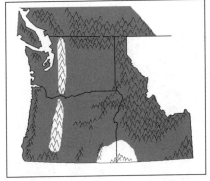

Hooded Mergansers

Location	Trend	Circles	Birds/100 ph
WA	7.8	33	10.48
ID	-4.5	15	104.18
BC	0.7	46	7.78
OR	4.1	43	7.70
ALL	1.3	1436	25.89

Swan Lake, Vernon, BC, in early winter). It is locally abundant at major lakes and rivers and in Puget Sound and the straits. Some birds remain to winter even at higher elevations in the Rocky Mountains of Idaho and British Columbia, as long as open water is available.

CBC data show an increase in the western part of the region and a slight decrease in Idaho.

Red-breasted Merganser
Mergus serrator

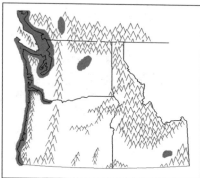

This merganser is common to uncommon along the coasts and in lower estuaries throughout the region. It is rare on fresh water away from the coast, but a few birds appear as wanderers in winter at lakes and rivers throughout the region. This species typically forms small flocks, not huge rafts, and is most common in estuaries and protected waters, less common on the open ocean. It is locally abundant in Puget Sound and the straits, where CBCs often record several hundred birds and is common to abundant at major estuaries along the outer coast.

It is occasional to uncommon at large lakes in eastern Washington and Idaho, but rare in eastern Oregon. It has

Location	Trend	Circles	Birds/100 ph
BC	0.6	38	3.20
WA	5.1	27	8.66
OR	-3.0	15	2.36
ALL	1.4	1078	19.89

concentrated at Banks Lake, Grant County, WA, and has been found on 37 percent of American Falls Reservoir, ID, CBCs, where it is significantly more regular than at most inland sites. It is increasing in winter in the Okanagan Valley, BC.

Ruddy Duck
Oxyura jamaicensis

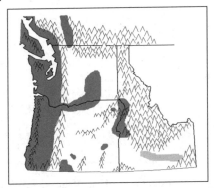

The Ruddy Duck is abundant to occasional throughout the region in winter on open water, though somewhat local. It is most common in Puget Sound, the straits, and the Klamath Basin, in southwestern British Columbia, at major estuaries, and locally along the Columbia River. It is regular but local in small numbers in the Okanagan Valley and in the Snake River valley.

In the western interior valleys of Oregon and Washington it is uncommon but widespread, appearing on sewage ponds, lakes, and reservoirs. It sometimes forms large flocks, so that there may be seventy-five birds on one lake and none on several nearby lakes or ponds that look equally satisfactory.

CBC data show a mixed trend with only Oregon having a slight increase.

Location	Trend	Circles	Birds/100 ph
BC	-2.6	21	6.39
WA	-3.7	33	9.79
OR	2.5	32	26.06
ALL	-0.1	1109	23.85

Order FALCONIFORMES
Family Accipitridae
Subfamily Pandioninae

Osprey
Pandion haliaetus

This species was formerly considered very rare in the region in winter, but today it is more regular, although still considered rare except in southwestern Oregon. It is now of annual occurrence in southwestern Oregon and in Puget Sound in winter, and birds have been found as far from those "temperate" zones as the Okanagan region of British Columbia, Wallowa Lake, OR, Moses Lake, WA, and eastern Idaho. In the early 1990s two to three birds wintered annually at Eugene, OR. It is still rare in winter along the southern British Columbia coast.

It is not clear why the species is now more regular in winter, but the most obvious possible explanation is that it has become steadily more common as a breeding bird in the past twenty-five years—there are simply more Ospreys breeding in and passing through the region.

Subfamily Accipitridae

White-tailed Kite
Elanus leucurus

The White-tailed Kite is locally common in western Oregon, and uncommon to rare farther north. This species was essentially unknown in the region until the 1960s, when the first outriders of a more or less steady influx appeared. In most of southwestern Oregon kites have become a fixture in the past twenty-five years, although populations fluctuate somewhat. The Rogue Valley, southern Willamette Valley, and the southern Oregon coast support the largest numbers. The species roosts communally at some sites such as Fern Ridge Reservoir, Lane County, OR, where as many as twenty have been seen at dusk, settling in for the evening.

The species now breeds locally at several sites in western Oregon, and additional birds appear to move in from California after breeding. Because this is one of the most visible and easily identified birds in the region, numbers reported on CBCs are probably quite accurate and reflective of actual numbers present.

The White-tailed Kite is still rare north of southwestern Washington, where it is regular in small numbers to Grays Harbor. It has not yet occurred in winter to far eastern Oregon or Washington or in Idaho, but these areas have records from other seasons and it may occur in winter in the future.

Location	Trend	Circles	Birds/100 ph
OR	5.4	15	0.10
ALL	2.9	195	0.61

Bald Eagle
Haliaeetus leucocephalus

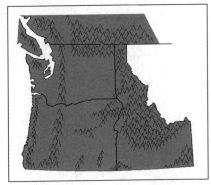

The Bald Eagle is common to uncommon anywhere that there is open water in winter. Birds tend to concentrate where there is plenty to eat, such as in Puget Sound and in the Klamath Basin, where hundreds gather each winter, in the Straits of Georgia (with concentrations of more than twenty-five hundred at Squamish), and at lakes in the Snake River and Salmon River valleys of Idaho. Eagles can be found at estuaries, along almost any sizable river, and at major

Bald Eagle

lakes. At many locations in the northern part of the region salmon runs result in major concentrations of eagles. When fish are not available Bald Eagles often dine on American Coots, a staple of their winter diet in much of the inland west (Cannings et al. 1987).

CBC data show an increase in all parts of the region, though nationally the species has showed no change over thirty years.

Location	Trend	Circles	Birds/100 ph
BC	4.5	45	6.37
ID	5.2	16	3.34
WA	5.0	35	0.76
OR	2.6	39	0.61
ALL	0.0	1295	1.20

Northern Harrier
Circus cyaneus

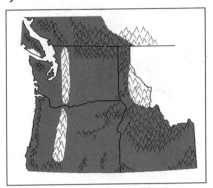

This bird is common to occasional throughout the region in winter. Harriers can be found using open country and marshland just about anywhere in the Northwest in winter. They concentrate below the snow line and in agricultural valleys and marshes, and along the coastal dunes. Numbers are highest in the western interior valleys and at coastal sites with large marshes, pastures, or other open country.

This species is rare in southeastern British Columbia and on southwestern Vancouver Island in winter and usually vacates the Okanagan Valley when daytime temperatures drop below freezing.

Location	Trend	Circles	Birds/100 ph
BC	2.2	29	0.67
ID	-3.7	16	2.90
WA	1.2	31	1.76
OR	0.8	43	3.89
ALL	-0.4	1712	1.88

Sharp-shinned Hawk
Accipiter striatus

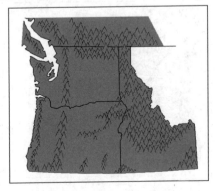

This small common forest hawk winters throughout the region. It is occasional in southeastern British Columbia in the Kootenay region but uncommon in wooded areas in the rest of the region. Perhaps because of observer bias it is often reported in cities in winter, but the availability of feeders

Sharp-shinned Hawk

stocked with juncos and sparrows may well attract birds to these areas. This species is less likely than the Cooper's Hawk to occur in open country. Availability of prey is probably the key factor— there are not many small birds to eat in desert riparian areas in winter. Sharp-shinned Hawks appear to withdraw from higher elevations in winter. An Idaho banding study showed that this species is present in the same urban areas in consecutive winters (Powers 1996).

Some observers speculate that this species is more often misidentified as Cooper's Hawk than vice versa (especially on CBCs where many inexperienced observers take part). CBC data show a slight increase in most of the region for Sharp-shinned Hawk and essentially even numbers for Cooper's Hawk.

Location	Trend	Circles	Birds/100 ph
BC	0.0	37	0.29
ID	1.9	15	0.34
WA	2.0	34	0.40
OR	0.9	42	0.32
ALL	1.4	1709	0.26

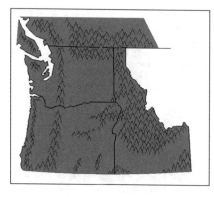

Cooper's Hawk
Accipiter cooperii

This uncommon hawk winters throughout the region but is less often reported on the outer coast. It is more willing to hunt in open areas than is the Sharp-shinned Hawk, but also remains in areas where roosting birds such as Rock Doves provide a ready food source. Accurate population estimates are not easily obtained, but it is generally believed to be less common in winter than the Sharp-shinned Hawk in most of the region. Like the Sharp-shinned hawks, these birds appear to withdraw from higher elevations in winter. See comment on identification under Sharp-shinned Hawk.

Location	Trend	Circles	Birds/100 ph
BC	0.0	32	0.27
WA	1.3	36	0.31
OR	0.7	42	0.35
ALL	0.8	1624	0.23

Northern Goshawk
Accipiter gentilis

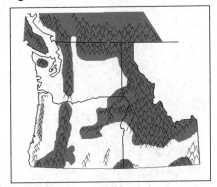

The Northern Goshawk is uncommon to occasional in forests throughout the region, and rare on the coast except in southwestern British Columbia, where it is occasional. Although this species is probably uncommon in the Cascades and Rocky Mountains at all seasons, it is not often reported in winter because, unlike its smaller cousins, it does not come down from the mountains in large numbers, perhaps because it takes larger prey, such as grouse, that also remain in the mountains in winter. A few birds are found every year in the foothills, lowlands, and coast ranges, but knowledge of the winter habits of the species is limited. The relative frequency of its occurrence in the lowlands of southwestern British Columbia and in the Rocky Mountain valleys of east-central Idaho may be a consequence of the nearness of extensive montane forests to these areas.

Cannings et al. (1987) note that when this species winters in the Okanagan Valley (where it is uncommon) its principal prey is Ring-necked Pheasant, but that it is an opportunistic hunter

Northern Goshawk

that chases a variety of species. Two-thirds of the goshawks reported wintering in the Okanagan are immatures, as are most of the birds reported in western Oregon and in the Lower Columbia Basin of southeastern Washington.

Location	Trend	Circles	Birds/100 ph
BC	0.3	34	0.14
WA	0.3	17	0.05
OR	-0.4	31	0.09
ALL	0.2	1007	0.11

Red-shouldered Hawk
Buteo lineatus

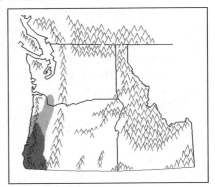

This species is locally common on the southern Oregon coast in winter, uncommon in the Rogue Valley, occasional elsewhere in southwestern Oregon, and rare elsewhere in the region. It has been expanding its breeding and wintering range into southwestern Oregon in the past twenty years, and is now regular in winter in Coos and Curry counties, with the Coquille Valley CBC finding steadily increasing numbers in the greatest concentration area of the species in Oregon. Winter 1996-97 saw a significant spillover of birds into northern Coos County, perhaps because the Coquille Valley had reached its carrying capacity.

It is also regular in small numbers elsewhere in southwestern Oregon, and is found annually north to the Corvallis area. It has been found more frequently in the northern Willamette Valley and along the central Oregon coast in the early 1990s, and seems to be continuing its expansion.

In Washington, there is one winter record of an adult at Nisqually NWR, Thurston County, from December 20, 1979, to February 23, 1980, and others at Ridgefield NWR, Clark County, in the winter of 1994-95 and 1995-96. More should be expected.

The species has not yet occurred in Idaho or B.C. in winter.

Red-shouldered Hawk trends on the Coquille Valley, OR, CBC	
1991	6
1992	10
1993	8
1994	10
1995	19
1996	24

Swainson's Hawk
Buteo swainsoni

There are no confirmed records of this species in winter in the region except for one probable winter specimen from British Columbia. This bird was collected "sometime between

November 1913 and February 1914 at Penticton" (Campbell et al. 1990, page 2:32.) There is one widely accepted record of an immature seen by numerous observers through late December 1968 at Fern Ridge Reservoir near Eugene, Lane County, OR (Gilligan et al. 1994), but I have been unable to locate any photographs of that bird.

There have been occasional winter reports in the region, and a few birds are now wintering at the Sacramento River delta in California. It is possible that some of the CBC reports are correct, but evidence is scanty.

Red-tailed Hawk
Buteo jamaicensis

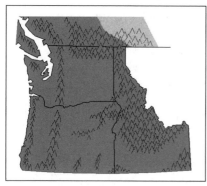

This is the most abundant and certainly the most widespread hawk in most of the region in winter. Many hundreds of these hawks winter in the western interior valleys and in open country throughout the region. Only in southeastern British Columbia are numbers typically low.

Birds concentrate in agricultural valleys where rodents are plentiful. They can also be found in almost any sizable opening in the forest where prey might be caught.

CBC trend data show an increase in every part of the region.

"Harlan's" Hawk, a well-marked subspecies, winters regularly in small numbers along the northern coast of Puget Sound around Bellingham. It is rare elsewhere in the region.

Location	Trend	Circles	Birds/100 ph
BC	4.1	40	1.07
ID	5.9	16	2.12
WA	5.7	35	3.88
OR	3.7	45	4.83
ALL	2.1	1936	2.90

Ferruginous Hawk
Buteo regalis

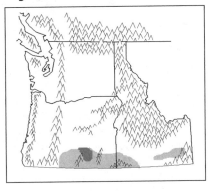

This hawk is uncommon to occasional in winter in the valleys of south-central Oregon and southern Idaho, and rare farther north except in the Lower Columbia Basin of southeast Washington, where it is occasional. It is of annual occurrence in winter in the lake basins and agricultural lands of south-central Oregon, and is rare but regular (not every year) in lowlands along the Snake River in Idaho and the Columbia in southern Washington. There is one record of a bird at Kelowna, BC, on January 10-16, 1979 (Campbell et al. 1989), and one in the upper Salmon River valley of east-central Idaho on February 21, 1972 (Roberts 1992).

West of the Cascades this species is very rare. In western Oregon it has wintered once at the Eugene airport and occasionally in the Rogue Valley. There are no proven reports from the Oregon coast although birds occur occasionally along the northern California coast.

It is likely that some CBC reports are of misidentified birds, so the status of this species in winter remains somewhat fuzzy.

Rough-legged Hawk
Buteo lagopus

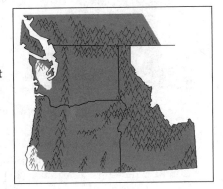

This northern buteo moves into the region every winter, but numbers vary markedly from year to year. In many years this species is abundant in the open parts of eastern Oregon, Washington, and British Columbia, and in Idaho. Most birds in British Columbia are in the Okanagan Valley, the Fraser lowlands, and at Creston, West Kootenays.

Location	Trend	Circles	Birds/100 ph
BC	3.6	20	1.30
ID	0.1	17	4.53
WA	3.0	29	0.92
OR	2.9	43	5.61
ALL	-0.1	1551	1.16

During years of major movement Rough-legged Hawks can also be abundant west of the Cascades south to the Willamette Valley, and common to uncommon elsewhere west of the mountains. This species is least common on the coast, even in good habitat.

During years in which smaller numbers appear, the species is still fairly common south into eastern Oregon and Idaho, but fewer birds reach the coast and the Willamette Valley. During these years the species can be absent from valleys south of Lane County, OR, and from much of the Oregon and Washington outer coast.

CBC data show an increase over thirty years throughout the region, although the irregular invasion habits of this species make short-term trends harder to detect.

Golden Eagle
Aquila chrysaetos

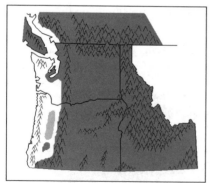

The Golden Eagle is common to uncommon and widespread east of the Cascades, with little winter movement or concentration except during periods of heavy snow, when birds may move down into the valleys. It is rare in northern Idaho in winter, as it is west of the Cascades, with a few birds present each winter in the western interior valleys, especially the southern Willamette Valley, where it is occasional. It is rare on the coast except in southwestern British Columbia and locally in northern Puget Sound, where it is occasional.

Location	Trend	Circles	Birds/100 ph
BC	-1.5	22	0.13
ID	-1.4	17	0.69
WA	-0.5	16	0.22
OR	-2.4	32	0.92
ALL	-1.0	722	0.41

CBC data show a decrease throughout the region. The reasons for this are not clear.

Family Falconidae
Subfamily Falconinae

American Kestrel
Falco sparverius

The American Kestrel is abundant in the western interior valleys and less common but widespread east of the mountains and on the coast. East of the Cascades, the largest numbers remain in the Columbia-Snake lowlands and in the lake basins of south-central Oregon. Snake River valley populations are thought to be less migratory 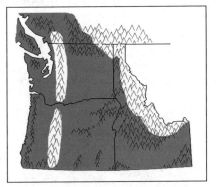 than other populations east of the Cascades (Henny and Brady 1994). It is uncommon in southwestern British Columbia and occasional in the interior. Most birds leave the Rocky Mountain region in winter. This species can be remarkably scarce on the coast.

Location	Trend	Circles	Birds/100 ph
BC	-0.5	33	0.40
ID	3.6	16	3.30
WA	0.6	36	2.01
OR	0.3	45	2.66
ALL	0.8	1909	2.59

Merlin
Falco columbarius

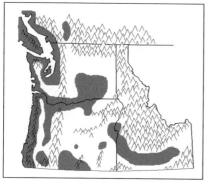

The Merlin is uncommon throughout the region in winter, found mainly near water. Although this species can be found along the coast and major waterways throughout the region, it remains uncommon to occasional except at major estuaries, lakes and reservoirs where a steady food supply is available. Some birds spend the winter in cities, feeding on pigeons, starlings, and other readily available prey.

Location	Trend	Circles	Birds/100 ph
BC	0.4	36	0.26
ID	-0.9	14	0.33
WA	1.5	31	0.20
OR	0.8	34	0.18
ALL	0.4	1067	0.13

Prairie Falcon
Falco mexicanus

This bird is uncommon but highly visible east of the Cascades in Oregon and southern Idaho, and occasional in southeastern Washington, where many birds withdraw in winter. It is occasional in the western interior valleys and rare on the coast and in northeastern Washington and northern Idaho.

This species remains in its desert and rimrock haunts for the most part, but a few birds move each year to the southern Willamette Valley, the Rogue Valley, and sometimes elsewhere. Very few birds reach the outer coast or the Puget Sound area,

Location	Trend	Circles	Birds/100 ph
ID	0.1	15	0.54
OR	2.5	30	10.44
ALL	1.5	488	0.28

where the species is rare. A few can be found north to the Okanagan Valley of interior British Columbia. It is a vagrant on the British Columbia coast with about five records in the Vancouver area.

Peregrine Falcon and shorebirds

Peregrine Falcon
Falco peregrinus

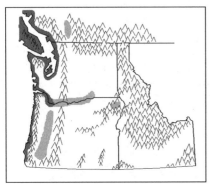

The Peregrine Falcon is uncommon to rare throughout the region in winter, progressively more rare farther east, with the great majority of records along the coast and at major rivers, lakes, and reservoirs. It is most common on the coast, in Puget Sound and the straits, and at adjacent lowlands where large numbers of ducks provide access to food throughout the season. For similar reasons, single birds can be found in the Okanagan Valley in winter in most years.

Except near water, this species is less likely than the Merlin to winter in urban areas, though in Seattle and Portland, resident pairs remain year-round.

CBC data show a slight decrease in British Columbia and increases in Oregon and Washington, where the species has become noticeably more common on the coast and easier to find inland.

Location	Trend	Circles	Birds/100 ph
BC	-0.1	23	0.11
WA	1.3	19	0.07
OR	1.1	24	0.08
ALL	0.0	666	0.05

Gyrfalcon
Falco rusticolus

The Gyrfalcon is occasional south to the Fraser lowlands, northern Puget Sound, the north end of the Okanagan Valley, the Kamloops area, BC, the lower Columbia Basin of southeast Washington, northeast Oregon, and the Idaho panhandle. It is rare south to central and eastern Oregon, southern Idaho, the

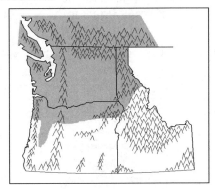

Willamette Valley, and the northern Oregon coast. Even in the Okanagan this is at best an occasional species.

Gyrfalcon

William Finley NWR, OR
January 22, 1995
Photograph by Skip Russell

Order GALLIFORMES
Family Phasianidae
Subfamily Phasianinae

Gray Partridge
Perdix perdix

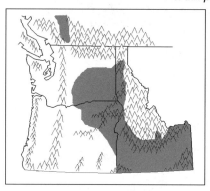

This resident introduced species can be found locally in most of lowland Idaho, locally in agricultural valleys in montane Idaho, eastern Washington, and northeastern Oregon. It can also be found in the Okanagan Valley, especially the northern part. It varies from uncommon to rare, and can be very hard to find along the edge of its range. These birds are most common in and adjacent to cultivated land. Numbers fluctuate from year to year. There is little movement in winter, but by the end of February they begin to form pairs.

CBC data from Idaho show a slight increase over time but elsewhere in the region the species has become rather spotty in distribution.

Location	Trend	Circles	Birds/100 ph
ID	1.9	15	3.84
ALL	-1.5	285	3.79

Chukar
Alectoris chukar

This bird is also introduced and is common in much of Idaho, eastern Oregon, eastern Washington, and southern inland British Columbia. It strongly prefers talus slopes, especially near streams, and is therefore most common in the rimrock areas that

Location	Trend	Circles	Birds/100 ph
OR	1.1	18	2.31
ALL	-0.8	99	1.43

are widespread east of the
Cascades. It is absent from the
agricultural areas preferred
by the Gray Partridge, except
where these abut preferred
habitat. There is some
flocking most of the year, but
there are no large winter
movements, although some
altitudinal movement occurs
in north-central Idaho.

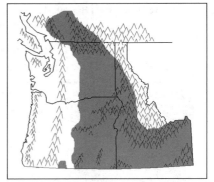

Ring-necked Pheasant
Phasianus colchicus

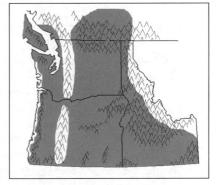

This introduced species is
common throughout the
region in the fringes of
agricultural lands, in brushy
areas, and even on the edge of
towns. It is least common and
locally absent along the coast
and absent from mountainous
areas. It can be locally
abundant, but without regular
stocking it does not survive
harsh winters at higher
elevations east of the Cascades. It is most common in the
western interior valleys and on the edges of agricultural areas
east of the Cascades, uncommon to occasional in valleys in the
coast ranges, occasional to rare on the coast.

CBC data show a notable drop in the region. This may be a
consequence of changes in stocking patterns, as the species is
not self-sustaining throughout the region.

Location	Trend	Circles	Birds/100 ph
WA	-1.4	34	7.02
BC	-3.2	25	5.07
ID	-1.3	15	25.95
OR	-3.6	40	11.30
ALL	-3.0	1208	9.67

Subfamily Tetraoninae

Ruffed Grouse
Bonasa umbellus

The Ruffed Grouse is common to uncommon in forested areas of the region; it can be found in both deciduous and coniferous woodlands of many types, and generally does not occur away from dense forests. It tends to move to coniferous forests in winter.

West of the Cascades this species sometimes occurs in heavy riparian woodland stringers in otherwise agricultural areas; this is usually not the case east of the mountains. Although this bird uses pure aspen groves in the northern part of its range in the region, it does not do so on isolated ranges in the Great Basin such as Steens Mountain and the ranges on the Nevada border. Large aspen stands are present there but grouse are not, except for recent introductions.

Although CBC trend data show a slight regionwide decline, finding grouse on CBCs is a hit-and-miss affair and these data should not be used for meaningful population trend estimates.

Location	Trend	Circles	Birds/100 ph
BC	-1.1	39	1.89
WA	-0.4	22	0.46
OR	-0.4	28	0.23
ALL	0.3	919	0.80

Sage Grouse
Centrocercus urophasianus

The Sage Grouse is a locally common resident in sagebrush areas of southern Idaho and southeastern Oregon and in central Washington. It was formerly rare to the extreme southern Okanagan Valley, but has now been extirpated. The species occurs in very few CBC circles in the region and is thus not often reported.

Likewise, its habitat is not well covered in winter. The limited data available suggest that its winter population has remained relatively stable nationally.

Spruce Grouse
Falcipennis canadensis

The Spruce Grouse is resident in British Columbia and in the Rocky Mountains of northern Idaho, the Wallowa Mountains of northeastern Oregon, the Selkirk range, and the Washington Cascades south to the vicinity of Mt. Adams. Very little is known about the winter habits of this grouse in the region, mainly because its preferred

habitat—subalpine fir, Engelmann spruce, and high-elevation lodgepole pine—is usually under many feet of snow. Far from descending from the mountains in late fall, this grouse typically moves up into the snow zone, where it winters within the canopy and survives on a diet of needles and whatever other vegetation it can find under trees. Its relative abundance is not well known.

Blue Grouse
Dendragapus obscurus

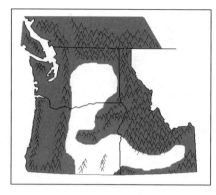

The Blue Grouse is resident in coniferous forests throughout the region. Its relative abundance is hard to determine, but, judging by the frequency with which observers find this species, it is probably uncommon throughout the region. However, as is true of other species that are hard to see, this bird is probably considerably more common than reports would indicate. Like the preceding species, Blue Grouse show reverse altitudinal migration in winter, moving up into the snow zone to feed and seek shelter among trees.

Location	Trend	Circles	Birds/100 ph
BC	·-0.1	17	0.10
ALL	-0.3	76	0.13

White-tailed Ptarmigan
Lagopus leucurus

This species is an uncommon resident in alpine areas of British Columbia, the Washington Cascades south to the vicinity of Mt. Rainier, and probably to the northern tip of Idaho. The Idaho Bird Records Committee considers this a review species that is hypothetical for the state, but there are at least thirty sight records from the Selkirk Mountains north of Sandpoint, ID (C. Trost, personal communication). An introduced population in the Wallowa Mountains of northeastern Oregon is now believed extirpated, and never supported many birds. The Oregon Bird Records Committee has removed the species from the state list.

Rock Ptarmigan
Lagopus mutus

This species barely enters the region in the coastal mountains of British Columbia. There are two lowland winter records, both photographed. One was in Vancouver from late November through December 5, 1975, the other was at White Rock January 9-18, 1976.

Sharp-tailed Grouse
Tympanuchus phasianellus

This grouse is uncommon to rare and a very local resident east of the Cascades in southern British Columbia, northeastern Washington, and southern Idaho. This species was formerly far more common and widespread throughout much of the Columbia-Snake region; today its distribution is confined to a few patches here and there in most of the region. It is widespread in appropriate habitat in parts of southeastern Idaho (C. Trost, personal communication). No native population remains in Oregon, although the species has been reintroduced in northern Wallowa County.

Subfamily Meleagridinae

Wild Turkey
Meleagris gallopavo

This is an introduced resident, locally common but more often uncommon or occasional. Most populations are restocked and therefore change in abundance rather abruptly. It is most common in central Washington, the Kootenay region of British Columbia, north-central, northeastern, and southwestern Oregon and locally in the Snake River valley and nearby foothills of Idaho.

Family Odontophoridae

Northern Bobwhite
Colinus virginianus

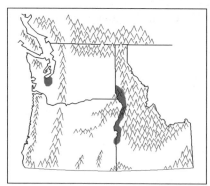

The Northern Bobwhite is an introduced resident, formerly uncommon to occasional in southeastern Washington, northern Umatilla County, OR, the Treasure Valley area of Malheur County, OR, and western Idaho. However, none have been reported since the severe winter of 1993 in southeast Washington (M. Denny, personal communication) and numbers appear to be declining throughout the region. It has probably been extirpated in Umatilla County, OR. It is occasionally introduced and reported elsewhere throughout the agricultural areas of the region.

Gambel's Quail
Callipepla gambelii

This species is present in the region only as a small introduced population in the upper Salmon River valley of east-central Idaho. According to Roberts (1992) it has been present in a 20-mile-long region since the initial introductions in 1916.

California Quail
Callipepla californica

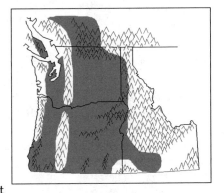

This is a native resident in southwestern Oregon, now common to abundant as an introduced bird in most of Oregon, Washington, and Idaho except in mountainous areas and extreme northeastern and southeastern Idaho. It is locally common in southwestern British Columbia and often abundant in the Okanagan Valley, where the Penticton CBC often reports the highest CBC numbers. It is occasional to absent along the northern Oregon coast and the outer coast of Washington and Vancouver Island.

This species often forms large coveys in fall and winter, with dozens of birds foraging and roosting together in brushy areas, where an incautious observer may produce an explosion of quail going in all directions.

Location	Trend	Circles	Birds/100 ph
BC	-2.2	16	30.02
WA	1.6	30	22.87
OR	-0.7	42	32.73
ALL	-1.6	237	29.84

Mountain Quail
Oreortyx pictus

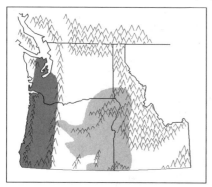

The Mountain Quail is a locally common to uncommon resident in the coast ranges and western Cascades of Oregon and the hills of southwestern Washington. It was formerly common to uncommon in much of the Blue Mountains, the Great Basin ranges, and western Idaho, but today it is declining, occasional to rare, and very local in this part of the region. It has not occurred in British Columbia except for an introduced population on southern Vancouver Island that may no longer be self-sustaining.

Location	Trend	Circles	Birds/100 ph
OR	-3.9	27	0.78
ALL	-0.9	79	0.84

Mountain Quail

Order GRUIFORMES
Family Rallidae
Subfamily Rallinae

Yellow Rail
Coturnicops noveboracensis

There is one winter record, a specimen collected February 1, 1900, near Scio, Linn County, OR. Larrison and Sonnenberg (1968) considered it casual in western Washington in winter, apparently on the basis of a single sight record regarding which little is known. This undated record is discounted by modern observers. Given that the species has been found in winter at Humboldt Bay, CA, and that its breeding range in south-central Oregon is larger than previously known, it is possible that a few birds winter in western Oregon, but their status is completely unknown.

Virginia Rail
Rallus limicola

This species is uncommon to locally abundant at marshes along the coast north to southern British Columbia. It is locally uncommon to occasional in the western interior valleys, especially the Rogue Valley, and occasional to rare east of the Cascades, mainly in the lake basins of south-central Oregon and at other lowland sites north locally to the Okanagan Valley. In mild years birds can be found in the Columbia-Snake lowlands east to southern Idaho. In most years a few birds can be found even well into the frozen areas of the region where warm springs or other factors keep habitat usable.

CBC numbers at marshes along the Oregon coast are often in the dozens, dropping off somewhat north to British Columbia, where numbers do not often exceed ten birds. Trend data indicate a significant increase regionwide in the past thirty

Location	Trend	Circles	Birds/100 ph
BC	1.8	16	0.10
WA	1.8	20	0.17
OR	2.7	24	0.30
ALL	2.1	609	0.23

years but much of this is likely due to the relatively recent availability of portable tape players and the inclination of observers to use them in winter in likely rail habitat.

Sora
Porzana carolina

The Sora is occasional to rare at marshes along the coast north to Puget Sound and in western interior valleys. It is occasional to uncommon annually in southwestern Oregon, with multiple birds often reported in the Rogue Valley and on the southern Oregon coast, and occasional in western Washington. It is rare (not annual) in British Columbia and east of the Cascades, but has occurred to the Okanagan Valley, Malheur NWR, and southern and eastern Idaho—even to the upper Salmon River valley—in winter.

The advent of small portable tape players in the past twenty years has no doubt resulted in a better understanding of the presence of this species in the region in winter (see Contreras 1992).

Common Moorhen
Gallinula chloropus

There is one winter record for the region, a bird at Winema Creek, Neskowin Beach, Tillamook County, OR, collected February 13, 1983. It is now specimen number S-8202 at the Carnegie Museum of Natural History, Pittsburgh.

American Coot
Fulica americana

The American Coot is abundant to uncommon throughout the region in winter, except at higher elevations; a few of these birds can be found almost anywhere there is still or slow-moving fresh water. Rafts of hundreds and locally thousands occur on the Columbia River and major lakes, where the species is 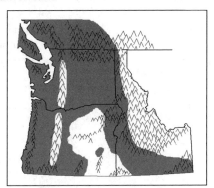 one of the main foods of Bald Eagles when fish are not available.

CBC numbers reflect the species' willingness to remain even in colder areas provided open water is available. However, trend data show a significant decrease in Idaho and a slight decrease in British Columbia and Oregon. Only Washington shows an increase.

Location	Trend	Circles	Birds/100 ph
BC	-8.7	34	71.89
ID	-7.1	14	1053.51
WA	1.5	35	71.55
OR	-2.1	41	24.02
ALL	-1.1	1407	111.08

American Coots

Family Gruidae
Subfamily Gruinae

Sandhill Crane
Grus canadensis

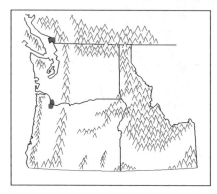

A small flock (fewer than a hundred birds) often winters at Sauvie Island, OR, and adjacent Ridgefield NWR, WA; otherwise the species is rare in winter, with most records from western Oregon and scattered early-winter records from Idaho and Washington. A few birds have wintered in the Fraser lowlands of southwestern British Columbia.

Migrant flocks typically arrive in the southern part of the region in late February.

Order CHARADRIIFORMES
Family Charadriidae
Subfamily Charadriinae

Black-bellied Plover
Pluvialis squatarola

This species is common in winter at larger estuaries throughout the region, uncommon to rare but widespread at inland locations west of the Cascades, mainly at larger lakes and reservoirs, sometimes in wet fields. Most of these birds

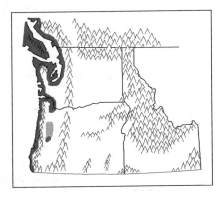

concentrate at such locations as Fern Ridge Reservoir near Eugene, OR, and the Sauvie Island, OR-Ridgefield NWR, WA complex along the Columbia River. The species is rare in winter east of the Cascades.

Numbers at favored locations range from a few to scores of birds. The largest concentration areas are Vancouver, BC, Puget Sound estuaries and Grays Harbor, WA, and the Columbia estuary and Tillamook and Coos counties, OR.

Location	Trend	Circles	Birds/100 ph
BC	-0.6	17	3.12
WA	-4.0	16	13.95
ALL	0.5	333	6.00

*Black-bellied Plovers and
Western Sandpipers*

Ramiel Papish 1996

Pacific Golden-Plover
Pluvialis fulva

This bird is rare in winter along the outer coasts and in the Fraser lowlands, where there are a few records of birds alone or with Black-bellied Plovers on mudflats, golf courses, and other such sites. The largest numbers reported in winter are nineteen at Comox, Vancouver Island, BC, on December 22, 1974, and a flock of eight on the Coos Bay, OR, CBC in 1979. These birds were presumably *P. fulva* although this species was not differentiated from the American Golden-Plover (*Pluvialis dominica*) at the time. There are two winter records from the Willamette Valley.

Snowy Plover
Charadrius alexandrinus

The Snowy Plover winters locally on the coasts of Oregon and Washington, with numbers substantially reduced from those found in the 1960s and 1970s. Some birds have been determined through banding to originate from populations breeding in the Great Basin and in California, as well as from local breeding populations.

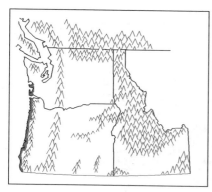

Semipalmated Plover
Charadrius semipalmatus

This plover winters along the outer coast of the region, with most birds from Grays Harbor southward. Numbers vary widely from year to year depending on weather conditions and presumably other factors; in some years only a few can be found at the major estuaries, while other years bring scores of birds, with the 224 on the Coos Bay, OR, CBC in 1992 probably the regional high count for winter. It is very rare in southwestern British Columbia in winter.

There is one inland winter record of seven birds at Malheur NWR, OR, on December 16, 1989.

This species strongly prefers broad mudflats, and is rarely found in other habitats.

Killdeer
Charadrius vociferus

The Killdeer is common to locally abundant in winter west of the Cascades, with numbers sometimes in the thousands in the central and southern Willamette Valley. It can be found in open fields with short grass or none, and on mud patches and gravel flats of almost any size, especially if wet.

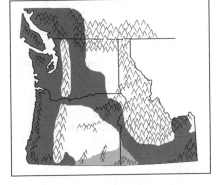

East of the Cascades this species remains in very small numbers in winter, confined mainly to lower elevations near open water, and is absent during severe winters. CBC trend data show a decrease in the region except in Oregon, where an increase has occurred.

Location	Trend	Circles	Birds/100 ph
BC	-5.6	41	1.59
ID	-5.9	17	3.19
OR	3.1	43	11.27
WA	-0.1	36	3.38
ALL	0.0	1551	6.53

Mountain Plover
Charadrius montanus

This is a rare vagrant in Oregon. Three of the six winter records were on the Corvallis CBC. Two were at the Corvallis airport on January 2, 1967; one bird was collected the next day (specimen in the Oregon State University collection), the other remained until March 10. Two birds were near Oakville, Linn County, on December 22, 1981. One was 3 miles south of Corvallis December 19-21, 1995, possibly the same bird that was reported from Ankeny NWR, Marion County, in late November 1995.

The remaining records are one at Siletz Bay, Lincoln County, on February 3 and 21-26, 1983; one on the beach near Tahkenitch Creek, Douglas County, on January 23, 1988; and two birds on the beach south of Bandon, Coos County, on December 6, 1989.

This species has not occurred in winter elsewhere in the region, although there are several fall records for Idaho.

Family Haematopodidae

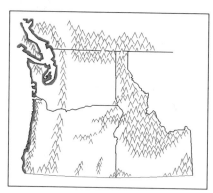

Black Oystercatcher
Haematopus bachmani

This bird is an uncommon but widespread and visible resident along the outer coast where extensive areas of rocks are available. It is locally absent or rare on the south-central Oregon coast and the central Washington coast where sandy beaches and dunes predominate.

Although this species does not migrate in winter, it does sometimes form large feeding and resting flocks at favored locations, where forty or more birds can occasionally be found.

There is one highly unusual inland record of a bird in distress captured at 3,435 ft. elevation at Bumping Lake in the Washington Cascades on January 8, 1947 (Nelson 1947).

Location	Trend	Circles	Birds/100 ph
BC	0.0	14	6.72
ALL	-1.1	56	3.07

Family Recurvirostridae

American Avocet
Recurvirostra americana

This is a rare lingerer in early winter. One was at Iona Island, BC, until December 4, 1986, and another was at Ladner, BC, in December 1995. Two were at Coos Bay, OR, on December 12, 1980. Two birds were at Klamath Falls, OR, from December 7 to 16, 1978, and two were noted at the 1979 CBC at Klamath Falls. One was at Lake Abert, OR, on December 2, 1994, and up to fifty-seven were there through early December 1995. A bird at Fern Ridge Reservoir, Lane County, OR, February 9-14, 1996, is the only mid-winter record for the region of which I am aware.

Black Oystercatchers

Family Scolopacidae
Subfamily Scolopacinae

Greater Yellowlegs
Tringa melanoleuca

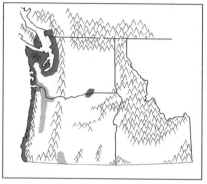

This bird is found in winter along the coast and locally inland west of the Cascades. It is occasional to locally common on the coast, where numbers are often highest in flooded pastureland and other backwaters far from the ocean. In British Columbia this species is uncommon on southeast Vancouver Island and occasional in the Fraser lowlands.

It is much more rare and local east of the Cascades, mainly in the Columbia River lowlands and the Klamath Basin, where a few birds can be found in most years. It is occasional in the Snake River basin in southwest Idaho. Severe winters force birds out of these areas.

CBC trend data suggest that the species is becoming more common in winter in Washington and possibly in Oregon.

Location	Trend	Circles	Birds/100 ph
WA	5.6	15	0.49
OR	1.4	16	0.40
ALL	0.6	544	0.87

Lesser Yellowlegs
Tringa flavipes

The Lesser Yellowlegs is absent from the region in most winters, with only a handful of proven records, though it may be somewhat more regular in recent years. Concerns regarding correct identification taint many CBC records of this species, but there are a few such records with adequate support, such as at Coos Bay, OR, in 1976 and Tillamook Bay, OR, in 1992.

Lesser Yellowlegs

*Summer Lake, OR,
December 26, 1996
(Photograph by Craig Miller)*

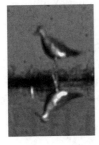

Lesser Yellowlegs

*Fern Ridge Reservoir, OR, winter 1995-96
(Photograph by Tom Mickel)*

The species is rare in southwestern British Columbia and western Washington in winter. The winter report from Walla Walla, eastern Washington, on December 16, 1990, has been unanimously rejected by the WBRC. It is absent from Idaho.

In the winters of 1994-95 and 1995-96 one or two birds could be found in the vicinity of Fern Ridge Reservoir, Lane County, OR. One was at Summer Lake, Lake County, OR, on December 26, 1996. Photos of these birds appear above.

In December 1996 one bird was in bottomlands along the Washington side of the Columbia River mouth. One bird was observed December 7, 1984, along the Malheur River near Riverside in Malheur County, OR (*American Birds* 39(2): 190), and there is one undocumented observation of a bird at Summer Lake, Lake County, OR, on December 18, 1986. These are the latest records east of the Cascades of which I am aware except for a documented record from the Klamath Basin.

Spotted Redshank
Tringa erythropus

One bird was at the south jetty of the Columbia River, Clatsop County, OR, from February 21 to March 15, 1981. It constitutes the only verified Oregon record.

Willet
Catoptrophorus semipalmatus

The Willet is occasional along the outer coast, mainly from Grays Harbor, WA, south. This species tends to use only favored estuaries, the most regular being Grays Harbor, WA, and Yaquina Bay and Coos Bay, OR. Birds are present more years than not at these locations.

It is rare in southwestern British Columbia and in Puget Sound.

Wandering Tattler
Heteroscelus incanus

This species is rare along the outer coast; it is a migrant along the Northwest coast and a few birds winter in some years. In most years tattlers are absent by late November and do not return until March, but in the winter of 1977-1978 about a dozen birds wintered between Tillamook and Gold Beach along the Oregon coast. There are no winter records away from rocky coastal areas. This species is extremely rare in southwestern British Columbia and in Puget Sound in winter.

Spotted Sandpiper
Actitis macularia

Most birds that breed in the Northwest depart by November, but a few remain each year, mainly along the coast and in southwestern Oregon, where the species is uncommon in small numbers. It is rare in southwestern British

Location	Trend	Circles	Birds/100 ph
BC	-0.3	15	0.06
WA	-0.3	17	0.12
OR	0.1	23	0.24
ALL	0.9	500	0.30

Columbia and very rare to eastern Idaho. There are two CBC records from Deschutes County, central Oregon.

CBC numbers show a steady increase southward. Bellingham found single birds three times during the period, while Portland found it on two-thirds of counts, averaging 1.2 birds, and Eugene found birds on every count in the period, with an average of just under five birds.

Upland Sandpiper
Bartramia longicauda

This is a vagrant. One was at Victoria, BC, from December 20, 1969 to January 4, 1970.

Whimbrel
Numenius phaeopus

The Whimbrel is rare in winter except from Yaquina Bay, OR, south. Whimbrels are fairly regular (usually fewer than five) at Yaquina Bay, Coos Bay and Bandon, OR, in winter. Fourteen birds at Yaquina Bay on the 1979 CBC is a regional winter high.

There are a few winter records from the coast of Washington and southwestern British Columbia, especially around Victoria, Vancouver Island. There are no inland winter records from the region.

Long-billed Curlew
Numenius americanus

The winter distribution of this species is similar to that of the Whimbrel, but it is somewhat less regular, being absent some years. Although there are no locations where the species is annual, it is seen most often at Willapa Bay, WA. Nine birds at Coos Bay on the 1995 CBC is the Oregon record (at least eleven were in the area), while the flock of fifty-five at Grays Harbor, WA on the 1994 CBC is the highest regional report. It is very rare to southwestern British Columbia.

Marbled Godwit
Limosa fedoa

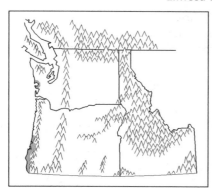

This is the most regular of the large shorebirds that winter in the region, and the only one that often occurs in sizable flocks. However, its winter distribution is irregular and unpredictable. In the 1970s this species was uncommon in winter at Coos Bay, OR, but it is now absent in most years. Flocks of fifteen to forty or more birds have occurred in winter at Grays Harbor, WA, and Tillamook Bay, Yaquina Bay, and Coos Bay, OR, with occasional birds elsewhere. It is rare to southwestern British Columbia.

There are two inland winter records. One was at Lower Klamath NWR, OR-CA, on December 3, 1978, and one was at Malheur NWR, OR, on February 28, 1991.

Ruddy Turnstone
Arenaria interpres

This species is present in small numbers in winter along the outer coast, especially from Tillamook Bay, OR, south. It is rare in Washington and occasional in southwestern British Columbia, though some birds occur in Puget Sound. In Oregon, it is almost annual on the Tillamook Bay CBC, and uncommon at Coos Bay and Bandon. It is much less regular at smaller estuaries and at Yaquina Bay. The Oregon and regional record was twenty-five birds at Gold Beach on the 1976 CBC.

This species often flocks with Black Turnstones in winter, but also feeds separately farther up bays in small rocky and muddy coves, sometimes on open mudflats.

Black Turnstone
Arenaria melanocephala

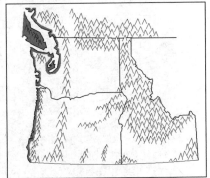

The Black Turnstone is common in rocky areas along the outer coast and sometimes farther up estuaries on log booms, exposed rocks, and, rarely, on mud flats. It is locally abundant where large expanses of relatively flat rocks are exposed at low tides. It is common inside Puget Sound to the Seattle area.

Location	Trend	Circles	Birds/100 ph
BC	1.1	22	20.63
WA	-0.8	18	4.93
ALL	-0.7	88	11.37

Surfbird
Aphriza virgata

This species is common in rocky areas along the outer coast, but uncommon in Puget Sound in similar habitat. CBC tallies can number in the hundreds at preferred coastal sites, but surfbirds are most often seen with turnstones as flocks of ten to forty birds. This species is less likely than its frequent companion the Black Turnstone to feed away from coastal rocks. See map for Black Turnstone on previous page.

The three "rockpipers" of the west coast:
from top to bottom, Rock Sandpiper, Black Turnstone, Surfbird

Photograph by W.E. Hoffman

Red Knot
Calidris canutus

Aside from the twenty-two birds that spent the whole winter at Pony Slough in Coos Bay, OR, in 1977, this species is rare in winter in the Northwest. It has been seen at Yaquina Bay, Tillamook Bay, and Bandon, OR, Grays Harbor, WA, and rarely to southwestern British Columbia. There are no reports away from coastal areas.

Sanderling
Calidris alba

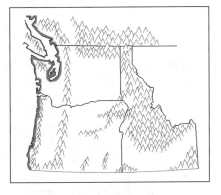

The Sanderling is common along sandy beaches, locally abundant. It is uncommon but regular in Puget Sound, with small numbers occasionally reaching Olympia.This is one of the most obvious shorebirds in the Northwest in winter, sometimes numbering in the thousands on open coastal beaches. CBC numbers fluctuate considerably from year to year at given locations, e.g., from 26 to 9,000 at Grays Harbor, WA, and from 31 to 3,118 at Tillamook Bay, OR. A few birds also occur with flocks of Dunlin, Black Turnstones, and other species, and can turn up on rocks, mudflats, and just about anywhere shorebirds go. The species occurs inland on occasion, mainly in fall migration. One was at Okanagan Landing, BC, on December 29, 1932.

Location	Trend	Circles	Birds/100 ph
BC	-1.9	19	24.18
WA	0.8	20	22.83
ALL	-1.3	329	12.10

Western Sandpiper
Calidris mauri

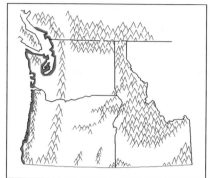

This species is occasional to uncommon at coastal sites, progressively more common farther south. It is generally rare inland, and usually absent east of the Cascades. It is rare in southwestern British Columbia and in southern Idaho.

The winter status of the species in the Northwest is obscured by the many CBC reports that may well refer to Dunlin. The decrease noted in the trend table may simply reflect that by the 1980s more observers were correctly identifying the species—that is, reporting fewer of them than previously mis-reported. The only locations where scores of birds can be found in most winters are Grays Harbor, WA, and Coos Bay, OR. Tillamook Bay, OR, also supports a few dozen birds in winter. Other than these sites, the species is occasional north of Grays Harbor (including Puget Sound) and elsewhere on the Oregon coast.

Unfortunately, CBC numbers and other shorebird census data generated by observers unfamiliar with the need to distinguish this species from Dunlin, Sanderling, and Least Sandpiper must be considered fuzzy. Despite this blurriness of records a few things are fairly clear regarding the distribution and abundance of Western Sandpipers in winter: they occur mainly at or immediately adjacent to saltwater sites. The only freshwater location where a few birds can be found in most winters is Fern Ridge Reservoir near Eugene, OR. The species is otherwise rare in the western interior valleys in winter.

Location	Trend	Circles	Birds/100 ph
WA	-1.2	19	14.63
OR	-1.7	17	5.02
ALL	-0.7	386	13.91

Least Sandpiper
Calidris minutilla

Unlike the Western Sandpiper, this species is reasonably well understood in the region, perhaps because it is more widespread, uses a greater variety of habitats, and is less likely to be confused with the larger sandpipers that are mostly confined to mudflats. It occurs in small numbers throughout the coastal parts of the region and is locally common at larger estuaries, where hundreds of birds are sometimes reported. It also occurs regularly in small numbers in wet areas in the western interior valleys, especially in the Willamette Valley.

It has been found in winter east of the Cascades on rare occasions. More birds remain there in mild years, with some to southern Idaho.

Location	Trend	Circles	Birds/100 ph
WA	-6.4	18	2.10
OR	0.1	22	4.29
ALL	-0.2	560	5.44

Baird's Sandpiper
Calidris bairdii

Although there are a few CBC records for this regular migrant species from the region, none are documented. The species normally does not winter in North America, and any reports from the Northwest should be discounted unless supported by a specimen or photograph.

Pectoral Sandpiper
Calidris melanotos

This regular migrant species has been reported in winter on occasion, but there are few documented records of its occurrence here. The only confirmed winter record for the region is from British Columbia: a bird was photographed at Burton, Lower Arrow Lake, BC, on December 19, 1988. One was at Chilliwack, BC, on January 3, 1927. A bird was at Campbell River on December 2, 1975, on the eastern side of Vancouver Island just to the north of the area covered by this book (all these records, Campbell et al. 1990). One was at Vernon, BC, on December 7, 1987.

Jewett et al. (1953) include one winter record for Washington, of ten birds on January 12-19, 1915, at Smith Island Bird Reserve. Two birds seen by experienced observers on the 1959 Portland, OR, CBC are considered an acceptable sight record. There are no generally accepted winter records for Idaho.

Sharp-tailed Sandpiper
Calidris acuminata

The only winter record of this late fall migrant is one at Iona Island, BC. on December 21, 1976.

Rock Sandpiper
Calidris ptilocnemis

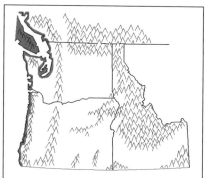

The Rock Sandpiper is uncommon and local on the rocky outer coast throughout the region, most common in British Columbia. This species usually occurs as single birds or small flocks mixed in with accretions of Black Turnstones or Surfbirds on the exposed coast, and rarely ventures far from the ocean. It is occasional in Puget Sound south to Seattle, uncommon on the Washington and northern Oregon coast, and occasional on the southern Oregon coast.

Location	Trend	Circles	Birds/100 ph
BC	-5.1	14	2.56
ALL	-5.8	34	1.12

Dunlin
Calidris alpina

This is the most abundant shorebird in the region in winter, approached only by Killdeer in the southern Willamette Valley. Grays Harbor, WA, is a major wintering area for this species, with an average CBC tally of about 30,000 birds and a peak count of 95,500 in 1977. Numbers have been reduced in recent years.

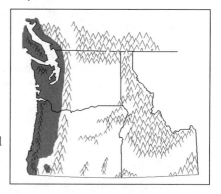

Counts at Ladner, BC, have reached 61,106 (1991). The Columbia River estuary, Tillamook Bay, OR, and other major coastal estuaries support thousands of these birds.

Dunlin also occur inland. The species is widespread in the western interior valleys, and several hundred birds are often in the Sauvie Island-Ridgefield NWR area. Similar flocks sometimes form in the central and southern Willamette Valley, often feeding in flooded pastures and grass-seed fields. Smaller numbers are seen in the Umpqua and Rogue valleys.

East of the Cascades a few birds can sometimes be found along major lakes and rivers when open water is available. The species is progressively rarer farther east but has occurred in southeastern Washington. It is extremely rare in winter in southwestern Idaho, mainly at Lake Lowell in Deer Flat NWR near Nampa.

Location	Trend	Circles	Birds/100 ph
BC	-2.6	24	118.36
WA	-4.1	24	263.85
OR	1.7	18	164.91
ALL	-1.9	479	32.70

Ruff
Philomachus pugnax

There is one winter record for the region, a Reeve on January 18, 1980, near Coquille, Coos County, OR.

Short-billed Dowitcher
Limnodromus griseus

This bird is very rare in the region in winter. Although there are many CBC reports, most are probably erroneous. The difficulty of distinguishing between the two dowitchers in basic plumage is considerable, and any winter record should be reported with details. There are a few generally accepted records for Washington and Oregon (calling birds). There are no confirmed records for British Columbia.

This species is rare but regular in winter north to Humboldt Bay, CA, and may well occur annually in the Northwest, at least on the Oregon coast, but its current status cannot be stated with certainty.

Long-billed Dowitcher
Limnodromus scolopaceus

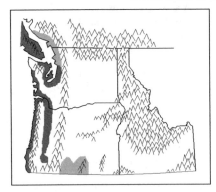

This dowitcher is locally common on the coast in winter; hundreds of birds can be found in the major estuaries of south coastal Washington and at Coos Bay, OR, and scores on other major estuaries. Numbers are lower in Puget Sound, where the species is progressively less common northward to British Columbia. It is less common inland, but quite regular in small numbers in the western interior valleys. It is generally absent east of the Cascades, but has occurred at Summer Lake and Klamath Falls,

Location	Trend	Circles	Birds/100 ph
OR	4.1	17	0.71
ALL	9.2	322	6.10

OR, on CBCs. In British Columbia, the species is rare in winter on the coast and absent from inland locations.

Away from the coast this species sometimes forages in flooded fields, along ponds and lakes, and in other situations affording soft ground to probe.

Common Snipe
Gallinago gallinago

This is one of the most widespread winter birds in the region, with CBCs west of the Cascades often reporting scores of birds, while small numbers remain in the colder areas east of the mountains. Snipe can be locally abundant, especially in coastal areas, when birds gather to feed in prime "muckland" such as the 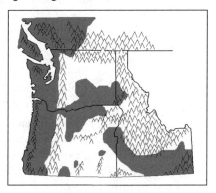 edges of flooded pastures, marshes, and similar sites. Single birds can often be found in ditches, along small ponds, and in other very small patches of boggy habitat.

East of the Cascades most birds are found along small waterways and springs or next to open areas on frozen lakes and river edges. Snipe can be found throughout the region in winter, but in severe winters may not be present in colder areas.

Location	Trend	Circles	Birds/100 ph
BC	-3.9	39	0.57
ID	-0.5	17	1.48
WA	-0.9	32	1.23
OR	0.8	44	2.65
ALL	-1.2	1466	1.37

Subfamily Phalaropodinae

Wilson's Phalarope
Phalaropus tricolor

This bird is extremely rare in winter. There are no accepted winter records for British Columbia. There are two CBC records for Oregon, of single birds at Coos Bay in 1976 and at Summer Lake in 1989. Documentation is not available for either record. There have been a few additional sight records. Northwest reports should be treated with caution unless confirmed by specimen or photograph.

Red-necked Phalarope
Phalaropus lobatus

Although this species has been reported in winter on CBCs in the region, these reports have never been confirmed by photograph or specimen. It is not expected in winter and records should be documented. Paulson (1993) listed no winter records for the region.

Red Phalarope
Phalaropus fulicaria

This species is a very late migrant off the west coast and some birds may winter to Northwest latitudes. As a consequence, this highly pelagic species can be found onshore and even inland in winter, mainly after storms. Under such conditions scores, even hundreds of birds can be found "wrecked" on the coast, swimming in puddles, standing in roads, and dead along roadsides. In mid-December 1995 thousands were blown ashore in Oregon and lesser numbers in southwest Washington.

Most records of significant numbers of birds occur along the Oregon coast, although smaller numbers sometimes come ashore in Washington and, rarely, in British Columbia, probably because of the timing of migration.

It is extremely rare east of the Cascades, with one record from Lake Abert, OR, on January 24, 1996.

Family Laridae
Subfamily Stercorariinae

South Polar Skua
Catharacta maccormicki

A single living beached bird on the Florence, OR, CBC in 1988 is the only onshore winter record for Oregon or, to my knowledge, for the region. Offshore status is not well known because of the limited number of trips in winter, but no records have come to light.

Pomarine Jaeger
Stercorarius pomarinus

This species is extremely rare along the coast in early winter. Single birds on the CBC at Florence in 1983, Yaquina Bay in 1986, Tillamook Bay in 1990, and one photographed near Astoria, OR, in January 1983 are the only winter records for Oregon. One was on the 1975 CBC at Grays Harbor, WA, and one was at Ilwaco, WA, on February 5, 1995. This migrant is rare off the coast in November and is likely to occur from time to time in December.

Parasitic Jaeger
Stercorarius parasiticus

The Parasitic Jaeger is extremely rare along the coast in winter. One was at Boundary Bay, BC on December 2, 1968; two were at Crescent Beach, BC, on December 8, 1976. A single bird on the White Rock CBC on January 2, 1978, is the only British Columbia CBC record. Single CBC records at Tillamook Bay in 1973 and Coos Bay in 1981 are the only winter records for Oregon. Several other reports of jaegers not identified as to species may relate to this species or to Pomarine Jaeger.

Subfamily Larinae

Franklin's Gull
Larus pipixcan

This bird is very rare in winter; there are fewer than ten winter records in Oregon, even fewer farther north.

Little Gull
Larus minutus

The Little Gull is very rare west of the Cascades in winter. It is rare but regular in Puget Sound in winter, less regular in southwestern British Columbia. One at Newport, Lincoln County, OR, on December 15, 1981, is the only winter record for Oregon.

Black-headed Gull
Larus ridibundus

This gull is very rare west of the Cascades in winter. Single birds at the Columbia estuary, Clatsop County, on the 1981 CBC and on the 1992 Tillamook Bay CBC are the only records for Oregon.

There are three Washington records of adult birds: one at Crockett Lake, Island County on December 20, 1987; one at Nisqually NWR, Thurston County from January 17 to 31, 1993; and one seen December 22, 1994, and March 9 and 19, 1995, at Point No Point, Kitsap County (Mattocks and Aanerud 1997).

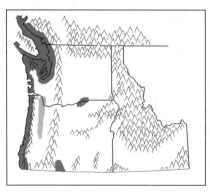

Bonaparte's Gull
Larus philadelphia

Bonaparte's Gull is abundant to occasional, mainly coastal, from Puget Sound and the straits southward. Most birds are found in the straits. Away from Puget Sound and the straits the species is far less common, with single birds or small flocks the norm, and no

Location	Trend	Circles	Birds/100 ph
BC	-0.1	20	2.87
WA	-3.1	23	23.51
OR	-1.5	14	1.21
ALL	5.6	778	19.64

birds at all at many sites in most years. It is less frequent in the western interior valleys than on the coast, but can be found occasionally at favored sites such as Fern Ridge Dam, Lane County, OR, along the Columbia River east to Portland, OR, and at other major water features.

East of the Cascades this species is absent in British Columbia, northeastern Washington, and eastern Oregon. There are a few records from Idaho (St. Maries and American Falls) in recent winters. It is rare in the rest of the region, but occasional along the Columbia River and in the Klamath Basin, where the Oregon CBC record of 151—unusually high for the area—was set in 1981.

This gull typically passes through the region in numbers in November and most birds are gone by December except in Puget Sound and the straits. Numbers vary considerably from year to year: Bellingham, WA, CBC has ranged from 3 to 511, Tacoma, WA, from 711 to 7280, Tillamook Bay, OR, from none to 13, and Coos Bay, OR, from none to 109.

Heermann's Gull
Larus heermanni

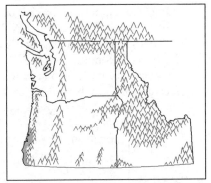

Heermann's Gull is occasional to rare along the coast in winter, mainly on the southern Oregon coast. This species comes north each summer along with the Brown Pelicans that it feeds with, and most birds of both species depart by mid-November. Heermann's Gulls are very rare in winter in Puget Sound and the straits, and only slightly more regular along the Washington coast. The species is not present every year at any site along the Oregon coast, and the only count where it is found fairly often is Coos Bay, OR, where it occurs on about one count in four, typically one or two birds. Coos Bay is also the only location on the Oregon coast where Brown Pelicans often remain into December.

In 1972 large numbers remained into mid-December and were tallied on CBCs, e.g. the 119 at Tillamook Bay, OR.

Mew Gull
Larus canus

The Mew Gull is abundant on the coast and locally in the western interior valleys in winter, but generally absent east of the Cascades. This gull winters by the thousands at some localities along the coast and in Puget Sound and the straits. In some locations, e.g., at Victoria, BC, Tillamook Bay, OR, and southern Puget Sound, CBC numbers can exceed ten thousand, while elsewhere, in Puget Sound and in the straits, numbers are more often in the hundreds and low thousands.

On most of the Oregon and Washington coast, the Columbia River east to Portland and locally in the Willamette Valley south to Eugene, this species is reported in the hundreds on CBCs. It is rare in the inland Umpqua and Rogue valleys. Mew Gulls often feed and rest on flooded or wet fields in winter, a habitat which is limited south of the Willamette Valley.

This species is rare east of the Cascades at any season, with a few records coming from the Okanagan Valley, the Columbia River east to southeast Washington and the Klamath Basin. In recent years, numbers along the Columbia have increased, with fewer than ten birds found annually along the Columbia River

Location	Trend	Circles	Birds/100 ph
WA	1.1	25	92.54
BC	-3.0	33	39.00
OR	0.9	21	51.34
ALL	-1.6	161	25.54

in southeast Washington (M. Denny, personal communication).
There are three or four winter records from Coeur d'Alene, ID.

Ring-billed Gull
Larus delawarensis

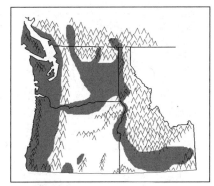

This is one of the most
abundant and widespread
gulls in most of the region in
winter, occurring along the
coast, in Puget Sound and the
straits, and along sizable
rivers, lakes, and reservoirs
inland to southern Idaho. It
reaches the northern edge of
its major winter range in the
Straits of Georgia and the Okanagan Valley.

This gull can be found anywhere from coastal estuaries to
local dumps and wet fields to fast-food parking lots. Numbers
are usually higher—sometimes much higher—inland than on
the open coast, with some of the highest CBC counts
(sometimes approaching a thousand birds) coming in eastern
Washington along the Columbia-Snake system and in the
Klamath Basin. It is also found offshore. The species is common
to abundant in winter throughout Idaho, where it is the most
common gull. It is uncommon to occasional north to the
Okanagan Valley (but abundant on Okanagan Lake), and can be
found locally in the eastern part of the region wherever open
water or garbage dumps permit.

Numbers are quite variable from year to year; counts at
Tillamook Bay, OR, range from one to 532, at Spokane, WA,
from none to 188, at Olympia, WA, from none to 163 and at
Penticton, BC, from none to 336. CBC trend data suggest a
continuing increase in numbers of this species.

Location	Trend	Circles	Birds/100 ph
BC	2.7	30	6.44
WA	1.4	31	13.43
OR	6.2	35	8.23
ALL	3.2	1465	57.06

California Gull
Larus californicus

This species has a similar winter distribution pattern to the Ring-billed Gull, but it is much less frequently reported in the colder areas east of the Cascades. This species is locally common to abundant where large flocks of gulls gather, especially in the western interior valleys and locally elsewhere in the Northwest. In most areas this species is significantly less common than the Ring-billed Gull; this is especially true on the coast and east of the Cascades, where this species can be hard to find except in large gull flocks. However, large flocks sometimes remain at open lakes in mild years, and many return by late February to the southern part of the region. Several hundred birds winter in the Lower Columbia Basin of southeast Washington. It occurs north to the Okanagan Valley in British Columbia; it is occasional to southwestern Idaho (annual on Boise CBC since 1990), rare to southeastern Idaho.

Location	Trend	Circles	Birds/100 ph
BC	1.0	23	0.77
OR	6.6	28	6.18
WA	-2.0	26	5.11
ALL	3.3	256	10.85

Herring Gull
Larus argentatus

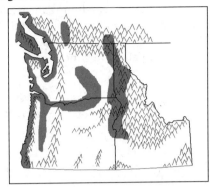

This species is widespread but not especially common in most of the region in winter. It is rather local, found in greatest numbers off southwestern British Columbia, at urban dump sites, along the Columbia-Snake river system, and at lakes and dumps in northern Idaho. It is notably hard to find in southern Idaho, most of eastern Oregon, and along the outer coast, where most CBCs find only a few birds. It is uncommon and local in the Okanagan Valley, and most depart in January when arctic weather moves in.

This is one of the least common gulls in coastal waters in the region except in British Columbia, where it is locally common. Many coastal CBCs held before the 1980s overreported this species because of observer reliance on field guides that did not accurately picture the northern race of the Western Gull, which more closely resembles the Herring Gull. These reports of scores and hundreds of Herring Gulls along the coast should be discounted. The downward trend data may reflect the greater accuracy of CBC gull identification in the past twenty years rather than any serious reduction in numbers of the species.

Limited information is available regarding the offshore status of this species in winter, but it is believed to be one of the commoner gulls far offshore. A pelagic trip out of Newport, OR, on January 29, 1994, found 120 birds feeding with other seabirds around a fishing boat 33 miles offshore, a number exceeded only by the two hundred Glaucous-winged Gulls.

Location	Trend	Circles	Birds/100 ph
BC	-6.1	42	11.30
WA	-4.6	30	5.69
OR	-3.1	20	6.30
ALL	0.1	1381	46.83

This species is uncommon and very local in the Willamette Valley in winter, found mainly around Eugene and locally elsewhere where dumps are available for foraging. It was common at Salem, OR, in the 1970s and 1980s, but is now occasional since the dump closed. It is rare in the Umpqua and Rogue valleys in winter.

Thayer's Gull
Larus thayeri

Thayer's Gull is locally abundant to uncommon, mainly west of the Cascades. The distribution of this species is still not well known, owing in large part to its relatively recent designation as a species by the AOU. It can be found west of the Cascades throughout the region, but concentrates with large gull flocks at preferred feeding areas such as dumps and certain estuaries, and can be uncommon to occasional elsewhere. Significant concentrations generating CBC counts in excess of a thousand birds can be found in northern Puget Sound and southwestern British Columbia. Lesser concentrations occur at Sauvie Island, OR. It is common to occasional in the Willamette Valley, mainly with concentrations of other gulls. It is very rare in the Umpqua and Rogue valleys.

East of the Cascades, this species is occasional to rare, and it is essentially absent in winter from far eastern Oregon and most of Idaho. In the Okanagan Valley and the Idaho panhandle it is occasional, found mainly with large flocks of other gulls.

Iceland Gull
Larus glaucoides

One was collected on February 22, 1965, at Coeur d'Alene, Idaho (Taylor and Trost 1987). There have been other reports for Washington, northern Idaho, and coastal areas of the region, but only two (not in winter) have been confirmed. A first-winter bird at Lewiston, ID, and Clarkston, WA, in December 1994-

January 1995 has been accepted as this species (Mattocks and Aanerud 1997). Another at Banks Lake, WA, on December 7, 1991, has also been accepted. Discussions continue as to whether this gull should be combined with other species and well-marked forms.

Slaty-backed Gull
Larus schistisagus

This Siberian species has recently been found a few times in the Northwest with large flocks of other gulls. At least two adults were photographed at Sauvie Island, OR, in the winter of 1992-93, and as many as four adults and two subadults were reported. One adult was present at the same location in the winter of 1994-95; one was present there in January 1996. One was at the Elwha River mouth, Clallam County, WA, from December 31, 1986, to January 4, 1987, and one was at Tacoma, WA, in the winter of 1995-96 (Tweit and Skriletz 1996).

There are at least six winter records from British Columbia. One was at Victoria on March 1, 1974. Single individuals wintered at the Burns Bog Landfill in Ladner from November 18, 1989, to February 25, 1990; October 27, 1990, to February 2, 1991, and December 27, 1993, to January 1994. Single adults were at Delta from November 18, 1989 to February 6, 1990, and on February 16, 1995.

The species is regular in summer in small numbers in Alaska and is likely to occur in the region again.

Slaty-backed Gull

Sauvie Island, OR
winter 1992-93
(Photograph © Skip Russell)

Western Gull
Larus occidentalis

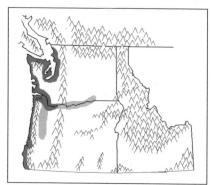

The Western Gull is abundant on the Oregon and Washington coast, uncommon in southern Puget Sound, occasional in the lower Columbia and Willamette valleys, and rare east of Portland, OR, on the Columbia River.

This is the most common gull on the Oregon outer coast in winter, with hundreds of birds found at most locations. It reaches the northern edge of its principal range on the northern Washington coast and in Puget Sound; it is progressively less common north to the northern end of the sound, where it is rare in Whatcom County, WA (Wahl 1995). It is uncommon to common off southwestern Vancouver Island but only occasional north to the Straits of Georgia.

Away from the ocean this gull is common to uncommon on the Columbia River east to Portland (mainly at Sauvie Island), occasional to rare with gull flocks in the Willamette Valley, and absent from the inland Umpqua and Rogue valleys.

East of the Cascades this gull can be found occasionally along the Columbia River east to southeast Washington, where it is now annual along the Columbia. Numbers are usually very low and the species is sometimes absent.

There are so many hundreds of hybrids, back-crosses, and possible intergrades between this species and the Glaucous-winged Gull in the Northwest that questions are often raised regarding the "purity" of inland "Western" Gulls. It is clear that a large number of Western and Glaucous-winged Gulls throughout the region, especially in Washington and northern Oregon, are of questionable pedigree. Nonetheless, some of the

Location	Trend	Circles	Birds/100 ph
BC	0.3	17	0.25
WA	-1.7	21	3.89
ALL	0.0	110	183.91

Western Gulls seen inland seem, visually, to bear characteristics of that species alone. In addition, birds on the southern Oregon coast seem mostly "pure" compared to those wintering, say, at the mouth of the Columbia.

Glaucous-winged Gull
Larus glaucescens

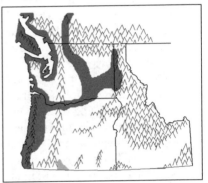

The Glaucous-winged Gull is abundant in Puget Sound and the straits, abundant south along the coast and inland on major rivers and lakes, and locally uncommon to rare east of the Cascades. This is the most common winter gull on salt water south to the southern Washington coast. From Tillamook Bay, OR, south, numbers of Western Gulls exceed numbers of Glaucous-winged Gulls, while thousands of hybrids of various generations cloud the concept of species and the determination of abundance.

Away from the ocean this gull is abundant east on the Columbia River to Sauvie Island, where it is usually the most common gull. It is common in the Willamette Valley, where it numbers in the hundreds on some CBCs where gulls congregate. It is occasional to rare in the inland Rogue and Umpqua valleys. It is uncommon to occasional east in the Columbia lowlands, with a few birds found rarely as far east as Coeur d'Alene Lake, ID.

This species has been increasing in numbers and expanding its range in the past twenty-five years. Breeding numbers on the west coast of British Columbia are estimated to have increased by 350 percent in the past thirty-five years (Butler et al. 1980, cited in Cannings et al. 1987) and the species has expanded its

Location	Trend	Circles	Birds/100 ph
OR	-2.7	21	28.87
BC	2.6	36	207.44
WA	-1.2	28	119.26
ALL	2.1	161	79.05

Eugene, OR, CBC	
Years	Average
1970-74	27
1975-79	96
1980-84	222
1985-89	117
1990-94	224

breeding range to northwestern Oregon and even islands in the Columbia River.

This expansion may have affected its winter range and abundance as well. Although numbers at the Tillamook Bay, OR, CBC have not changed significantly in thirty years, more birds are found today on inland CBCs. Note the changes on the Eugene, OR, CBC. This table does not include the significant increase in large pink-footed gulls treated as hybrids.

East of the Cascades, this gull is common along the Columbia River east to John Day Dam and uncommon east to McNary Dam and the Tri-Cities, WA, area. It is very rare farther east, with a few records for the Idaho Panhandle. One was at Malheur NWR, OR, on December 19, 1988, and at Farewell Bend (Baker/Malheur counties) on the Oregon side of the Snake River on November 16, 1987 (Gilligan et al. 1994). It is occasional but increasing in the Okanagan Valley, and occasional to rare in the Klamath Basin and along major rivers and lakes in eastern Washington in winter.

Ambiguous CBC trend data may reflect the fact that observers today are more willing to report large numbers of gray-winged pink-footed gulls as hybrids rather than as Glaucous-winged Gulls.

Glaucous Gull
Larus hyperboreus

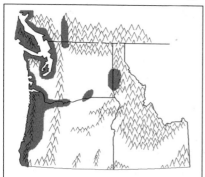

This northern gull moves into the Northwest in small numbers every winter. It tends to be found where gulls congregate, perhaps because observers also congregate there. As a consequence there are more records for areas with easily watched dumps and resting areas than for places where birds must be found as they fly by.

That caveat noted, Glaucous Gulls are almost annual at regularly covered sites in coastal British Columbia (where it is

Location	Trend	Circles	Birds/100 ph
BC	-1.6	27	0.62
ALL	5.3	458	12.76

uncommon), the Okanagan Valley, at concentration areas in the Idaho panhandle, at Sauvie Island, in the lower Columbia Basin in southeast Washington, and along the northern Oregon coast. They are progressively less common farther south along the Oregon coast, occasional to rare in the southern Willamette Valley, and very rare to absent from eastern Oregon and southern Idaho. The species is also oddly rare in Puget Sound and along the Washington coast. The reasons for this patchy winter distribution, other than as noted above, are not clear.

Black-legged Kittiwake
Rissa tridactyla

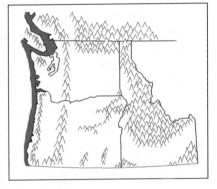

This species is uncommon to rare along the outer coast in early winter, but concentrations are sometimes noted, especially in Oregon. It is found on two years out of three at most CBC locations on the outer Oregon coast, but is much less common farther north and is very rare in the straits and in Puget Sound. Numbers on the outer coast are normally small—fewer than five birds at a given CBC—but in peak years large numbers have been found, e.g, 165 at Yaquina Bay, OR, in 1986, 54 at Florence, OR, in 1983, and 40 at Grays Harbor, WA, in 1977.

The fact that this species is far more common in early winter along the Oregon coast than farther north, yet seems, from limited pelagic trip data, absent offshore in January, suggests that it is a very late fall migrant like the Red Phalarope, and that the large number of birds sometimes found in December represents the tail end of migration rather than a sizable offshore wintering population.

The species is extremely rare east of the Cascades in winter. A specimen was collected near Howe, ID, on February 13, 1980. It is now specimen no. 80-233 at the Conner Museum at Washington State University. One was found on the Snake River near Clarkston, WA, on February 29, 1976 (*American Birds* 30(3): 743), and one was below John Day Dam, Sherman County, OR, on December 5, 1995.

Red-legged Kittiwake
Rissa brevirostris

This little-known species is rare offshore in winter, and is known mainly from occasional mid-winter washups and a few onshore records. There is one generally accepted Oregon CBC record, at the Coos Bay jetties on the 1988 count (details for this record and unpublished count are on file with the regional CBC editor), and records accepted by the OBRC are noted below:

Sunset Beach, Clatsop County, one decomposed bird found on January 24, 1982. DeLake [D Lake], Lincoln County, one found dead on the beach on January 28, 1933 (Specimen number USNM 589514 [originally number 2200] at United States National Museum). Cannon Beach, Clatsop County, one found dead on the beach on December 30, 1981 (unsexed specimen is number UWBM 39589 at the Burke Museum, University of Washington, Seattle). Rockaway Beach, Tillamook County, one winter plumaged adult moribund on beach January 16, 1989. One was reported December 3, 1995, 40 miles west of Tillamook, Tillamook County (*Oregon Birds* 22(3): 95).

There are at least three records for Washington. One adult was found dead at Lake Ozette, Clallam County, on December 1, 1978 (specimen number TESC 207 at the Evergreen State College), and one was seen off Westport, Grays Harbor County, on January 19, 1991. The first Washington record was near Leadbetter Point, Pacific County, on January 27, 1974 (Tweit and Skriletz 1996).

Ivory Gull
Pagophila eburnea

This bird is an extremely rare vagrant from the Arctic. There is one record from Victoria, BC, on February 19, 1925, and one winter record for Washington, December 20, 1975, at Grays Harbor.

Ross' Gull
Rhodostethia rosea

This rare arctic vagrant has appeared in the region only a few times. One adult was photographed at Yaquina Bay, Lincoln County, OR, and was present from February 18 to March 1, 1987. Another was at McNary Dam, OR and WA, from November 27 to December 1, 1995. One was photographed at Victoria, BC, on November 9, 1966.

Ross's Gull

*McNary Dam, WA-OR, 1995
(Photograph by Ruth Sullivan)*

Sabine's Gull
Xema sabini

This species is extremely rare in winter along the outer coast. Oregon has two CBC records: an immature seen by the author off Cape Arago on the 1978 Coos Bay CBC, and a bird seen on the 1987 Coos Bay CBC. One was seen on the 1995 Tillamook Bay CBC and another December 15, 1979, at the south jetty of the Columbia River. These no doubt represent very late migrants, as the species has been found a number of times in western Oregon in November. A recently dead bird was on the beach at Newport, Lincoln County, OR, December 4, 1995. One was well described on the Port Townsend, WA, CBC in 1995. An early migrant was at Yaquina Bay February 22, 1992.

It is very rare in southwestern British Columbia waters in winter; one was found at Salmon Arm in the Shuswap Valley just north of the Okanagan Valley, during the 1995 CBC.

Subfamily Sterninae

Forster's Tern
Sterna forsteri

A single bird on December 13, 1995, at Bandon, OR, after a series of strong southerly windstorms is the only record of which I am aware for Oregon. Single birds were reported on the Tri-Cities, WA, CBC in 1970 and 1974 for the only CBC records in Washington. There have been no winter reports from Idaho or British Columbia.

Black Tern
Chlidonias niger

An intriguing report of a Black Tern standing on the beach at the 1979 Columbia Estuary CBC is the only known winter record for the region. Although the bird was seen by an observer familiar with the species, the possibility that this bird was actually of a wind-blown Asiatic species, i.e. White-winged Tern, cannot be ruled out.

Family Alcidae

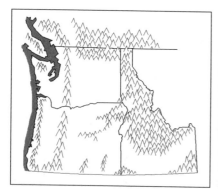

Common Murre
Uria aalge

The Common Murre is locally abundant along the outer coast and ocean and in the straits. Numbers fluctuate greatly from year to year, and birds can be absent in some areas, while total counts at favored coastal sites can range into the tens of thousands in peak years. This species often comes into lower estuaries and many are found in Puget Sound.

Location	Trend	Circles	Birds/100 ph
BC	-2.2	26	43.47
WA	4.4	20	111.52
ALL	-5.9	134	80.13

Thick-billed Murre
Uria lomvia

This murre is very rare along the coast. There are no winter records for southern British Columbia. In Washington, there are four confirmed winter sightings. One was at San Juan Island, San Juan County, on December 6, 1979; two were at Ocean Shores, Grays Harbor County, on December 15, 1979; one was sighted at Drayton Harbor, Whatcom County, on December 31, 1986; and one was off Westport, Grays Harbor County, on

January 20, 1990. In addition, there are two beached specimens from Washington: an adult male found at Westport on February 19, 1933 (specimen number UWBM 11633 at Burke Museum, University of Washington), and one killed by an oil spill off Anderson Point, Clallam County, in December 1988 (specimen number UWBM 42970) (Tweit and Skriletz; Tweit and Paulson).

In Oregon there are two confirmed winter records. One was found dead on the beach near Mercer, north of Florence, Lane County, on January 30, 1933 (Scott and Nehls 1974). This bird is now specimen number 10,483 in the Oregon State University collection. Another was found dead at Depoe Bay, Lincoln County, on January 14, 1933. The specimen is number 9258 at the Yale Peabody Museum, New Haven, Connecticut.

Pigeon Guillemot
Cepphus columba

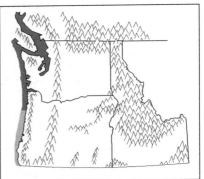

This bird is locally abundant in the straits off British Columbia and uncommon to occasional along the coast and in Puget Sound, usually in very small numbers. However, concentrations do appear, e.g. the 1,149 on the 1988 Sequim-Dungeness, WA, CBC. It is often rare to absent in winter south of northern Washington. Most probably winter far at sea. This species sometimes winters in small numbers in lower estuaries along the outer coast.

Location	Trend	Circles	Birds/100 ph
BC	-2.5	21	1.19
WA	3.6	19	8.97
ALL	-0.4	69	1.63

Marbled Murrelet
Brachyramphus marmoratus

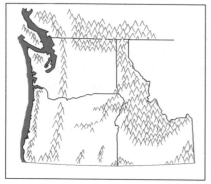

This species is uncommon and local along the coast and common to occasional in Puget Sound and the straits. It tends to use certain locations along the coast in winter, and only occasionally comes into estuaries. Numbers are rarely large, with a few pairs found on the water off many headlands near breeding grounds. Concentrations can be found in the straits and northern Puget Sound and along the west side of Vancouver Island. The species is harder to find where there are no nearby breeding sites, such as off Coos and northern Curry counties, OR. The status of the recently split Long-billed Murrelet (*B. perdix*) in the region in winter is unknown.

Location	Trend	Circles	Birds/100 ph
BC	0.9	24	6.09
WA	4.3	21	4.64
ALL	1.2	76	2.87

Marbled Murrelet

Kittlitz's Murrelet
Brachyramphus brevirostris

There have been two winter records for the region. One spent the winter of 1985-86 near Victoria, BC (Campbell et al. 1990), and another was at Friday Harbor in the San Juan Islands, WA, on January 4, 1974 (Mattocks et al. 1976).

Xantus' Murrelet
Synthliboramphus hypoleucus

One was collected on December 6, 1941, at Copalis Beach, Grays Harbor County, WA (Mattocks et al. 1976).

Ancient Murrelet
Synthliboramphus antiquus

This murrelet winters along and off the coast; numbers vary widely by location and from year to year. Large rafts often form in the straits and northern Puget Sound, and the 6,401 seen on the Victoria, BC, CBC on December 30, 1973, remains the all-time North American record.

Hundreds can be seen passing Point No Point, Kitsap County, WA, in December. On January 29, 1994, 480 birds were seen on a pelagic trip out of Newport, OR, with three hundred of these from 13 to 20 miles out. The largest number ever found on an Oregon CBC is 1,004 (Coquille Valley, 1995), but normally no more than one to two hundred birds are found at coastal Oregon sites in peak years, and in some years the species is absent. This species is considered by most observers to be significantly more common close-in along the Oregon coast in the past ten years, with numbers five to ten times higher than those found in the 1970s and 1980s.

This bird is a vagrant inland as far as Idaho.

Cassin's Auklet
Ptychoramphus aleuticus

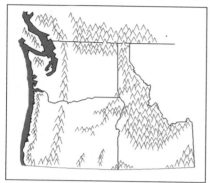 This species is common offshore, occasional within sight of shore. It is most regular in British Columbia off the western side of Vancouver Island. Although most of these birds stay out of sight of land-based observers, some can be seen from coastal headlands. A careful observer watching under good conditions with a scope can usually find this species (albeit probably in flight); sometimes birds come in as close as between jetties. Offshore status is based on relatively few pelagic trips. Thirty were noted on a pelagic trip out of Newport, OR, on January 29, 1994.

Parakeet Auklet
Aethia psittacula

This is a rare wanderer. Most of these birds winter off Alaska, but there have been a number of washups on Northwestern beaches, and occasionally a live bird is seen from a boat.

In Washington, one was seen between Port Townsend and Cape Flattery on January 15, 1907, and one was at Westport on December 18, 1934 (Jewett et al. 1953). Another was at Grayland, Pacific County, on February 21, 1937 (Paulson 1995). A recent record is from February 26, 1990, at Grayland, Grays Harbor County (Tweit and Skriletz 1996).

Seven winter records are accepted by the OBRC. Tillamook Bay, Tillamook County, one dead on the beach on December 3, 1977. Sunset Beach, Clatsop County, three found dead on the beach on February 23, 1933 (a male specimen is museum number 21869, a female is number 21870, and 1 of unknown sex is number 21871 at the Natural History Museum, San Diego, California). Netarts Bay, Tillamook County, one female found dead on the beach on January 1, 1913 (specimen is museum number 21872 at the Natural History Museum, San Diego, California), first verified Oregon record. Newport, Lincoln County, one male found dead on the beach on January 17, 1914 (specimen is number 21873 in the Natural History Museum, San Diego, California). Delake, Lincoln County, one male found dead on the beach on February 5, 1933 (specimen is number 21874 at the Natural History Museum, San Diego, California). Gleneden, Lincoln County, one of unknown sex found dead on the beach on February 26, 1933 (specimen is number 21875 at the Natural History Museum, San Diego, California). Taft, Lincoln County, one female found dead on the beach February 21, 1932 (specimen is number 21876 at the Natural History Museum, San Diego, California).

Rhinoceros Auklet
Cerorhinca monocerata

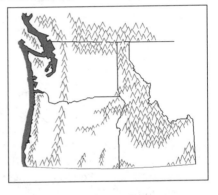

This species is common to abundant in Puget Sound (especially the central and southern portion) and locally in the straits in winter, more local along the outer coast. It is rare in winter in the Bellingham, WA, area (Wahl 1995) and uncommon along the outer coast of the entire region, except occasional on the southern Oregon coast. It is locally common at favored sites, often near nesting grounds, e.g., off northwestern Washington and the central Oregon coast.

Location	Trend	Circles	Birds/100 ph
WA	-0.2	17	2.21
ALL	15.6	58	67.04

Tufted Puffin
Fratercula cirrhata

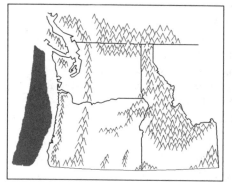

Most Tufted Puffins winter far offshore and are not reported. The species is rare offshore Vancouver Island. The only sizable number reported in the region is forty-five birds with twenty-five thousand Common Murres and other alcids during the El Niño winter of 1976 off Cape Arago, Coos County, OR. Occasional washups are found.

Horned Puffin
Fratercula corniculata

This puffin winters in numbers far offshore (200 or more miles out) but reports are few, and most refer to beached individuals. It is rare off Vancouver Island. There is one record of a living bird from Puget Sound off Kingston, Kitsap County, WA, on December 15, 1991.

In some winters freshly dead birds wash up on the region's beaches, and in the winter of 1932-33 several hundred dead birds washed up.

Order COLUMBIFORMES
Family Columbidae

Rock Dove
Columba livia

The Rock Dove is abundant to uncommon throughout the region except in forested areas. Most birds concentrate in cities, around farmsteads, and in rimrock east of the Cascades, especially near areas where grain is available for food. The extent to which this species concentrates or moves around from season to season is not clear, but there

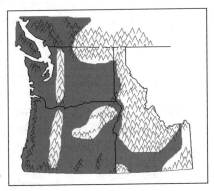

appears to be some withdrawal from higher elevation areas in winter.

Band-tailed Pigeon
Columba fasciata

This species has one of the most patchy winter distributions of any in the region. Although it breeds west of the Cascades north to the southern tip of the Alaska panhandle, most of these birds withdraw in winter. Those that remain tend to concentrate in the southwestern British Columbia and Puget Sound

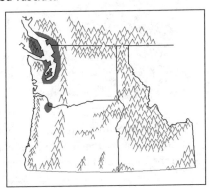

area, with other pockets in Portland, OR, and, some years, in southwestern Oregon.

It can be common in some years in the Puget Sound area and on southeastern Vancouver Island, but is usually uncommon to rare elsewhere. In most years it is not reported on CBCs in areas where it is a common breeder.

Location	Trend	Circles	Birds/100 ph
BC	2.2	16	2.26
WA	-3.3	20	3.06
OR	-1.0	18	1.03
ALL	0.8	186	2.88

There is one winter record from eastern Oregon at Adams, Umatilla County, on February 17-26, 1990.

White-winged Dove
Zenaida asiatica

This is a vagrant. One winter record, a bird found on the Tillamook Bay, OR, CBC on December 20, 1986, has been accepted by the OBRC.

Mourning Dove
Zenaida macroura

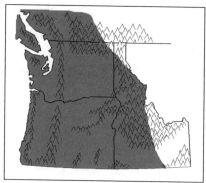

The Mourning Dove is common to abundant in open country and open woodland where grain or other food sources are available, but uncommon in British Columbia. Many remain in winter even in the colder inland parts of the region, especially in the agricultural lowlands of the Snake-Columbia river system. It is much less common in coastal areas, where it can be difficult to find. It is often absent in winter along the northern coast of Puget Sound and generally absent from forested areas.

Location	Trend	Circles	Birds/100 ph
BC	-2.2	21	4.51
WA	-3.0	26	4.50
OR	0.0	38	5.48
ALL	2.3	1860	18.63

Order Psittaciformes
Family Psittacidae

Monk Parakeet
Myiopsitta monachus

A small colony of these birds exists at the Portland, OR, airport and in nearby areas. It is not clear whether the population is self-sustaining.

Order STRIGIFORMES
Family Tytonidae

Barn Owl
Tyto alba

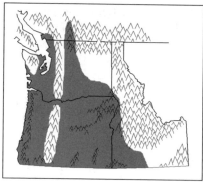

The Barn Owl is uncommon to occasional, mainly at lower elevations. As is true of most owls, abundance is speculative owing to the species' nocturnal habits and limited field research in winter. It is absent from inland and northern British Columbia, northeastern Washington, and the Rocky Mountain region of Idaho, but is a rare winter resident in the Okanagan Valley north to Vernon in recent years. It may be expanding its winter range and abundance in the lower Columbia Basin of southeast Washington, the Snake River lowlands of southwestern Idaho, and far eastern Oregon. See Contreras and Kindschy (1996) for discussion of the latter region. Range is thought to be limited by the severity of winters (mainly snowpack) that restrict its ability to hunt in its preferred open country.

It is most common in agricultural areas, lowland pastures, and other relatively large open spaces, but less common on the coast, where it concentrates in areas where there is significant agricultural land. It is generally absent from forested areas and higher elevations.

Location	Trend	Circles	Birds/100 ph
WA	0.8	23	0.19
OR	1.7	30	0.22
ALL	0.5	718	0.13

Family Strigidae

Western Screech-Owl
Otus kennicottii

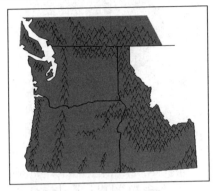

This species is common to occasional throughout the region except in dense coniferous forests. It is occasional in southeastern Idaho. This owl is one of the most adaptable and cosmopolitan of those that winter in the region. It occurs in all manner of habitats that provide access to mice and voles, such as tree-lined pastures, small clearings in open forest, desert canyons, city parks, and many others, though it generally stays away from dense forests except where there are openings.

Because of this species' nocturnal habits and the great variation in owling effort among CBCs, estimates of relative density across the region are hard to make. The solid upward trend in CBC data certainly represents changes in observer effort in the past thirty years rather than any change in population.

Location	Trend	Circles	Birds/100 ph
BC	1.5	14	0.08
WA	2.9	21	0.07
OR	2.0	29	0.12
ALL	2.1	206	0.07

Great Horned Owl
Bubo virginianus

The Great Horned Owl is common throughout the region in a wide variety of habitats. It is especially obvious in winter east of the Cascades, where nesting is underway by January (in the southern part of the region) or February (in British Columbia) while trees are still bare. Relative abundance is not well known owing to the species' nocturnal habits and the lack of winter research. The upward trend of CBC data is probably related to observer effort rather than a change in population.

Location	Trend	Circles	Birds/100 ph
BC	0.3	27	0.30
ID	1.0	18	0.55
WA	1.7	30	0.26
OR	2.9	45	0.85
ALL	1.7	1835	0.72

Snowy Owl
Nyctea scandiaca

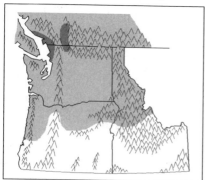

This is an irruptive wanderer that enters the region from the arctic. Abundance varies markedly depending on whether it is an "invasion" year—a year in which the lemming population in the arctic crashes and birds come south for food. Because this species prefers large expanses of open country, it can be more common south of British Columbia than in

Location	Trend	Circles	Birds/100 ph
WA	-3.4	14	0.08
ALL	-0.4	540	1.58

the province even though it moves in from the north. However, the open country of the Fraser lowlands is a favorite area, and the all-time record of 107 birds on a CBC was set at Ladner on December 22, 1973.

This species occurs about every three years at Bellingham, WA, and about every six or seven years in most of the rest of Washington, inland British Columbia, northern Oregon, and Idaho, although it is annual in eastern Washington, often at Pot Holes Reservoir, Grant County, or in Lincoln County. Even in peak years it rarely occurs south of the southern end of the Willamette Valley or the central Oregon coast. In the biggest invasion year of the past twenty-five years (1973-74), thirty-two birds reached Bellingham, WA, and eleven were found at Tillamook Bay, OR. The winter of 1996-97 also brought high numbers. However, most years bring only single birds here and there.

In a typical movement year that brings only small numbers of birds, very few pass south of the Columbia River plains, with Clatsop Spit at the river's mouth sometimes the only place that an owl settles for the season as far south as Oregon. East of the Cascades very few birds pass the Blue Mountain ridges, and most birds settle for the season in the Columbia bottomlands and nearby wheat fields. Occasional birds have reached southern Idaho.

Birds that winter in coastal areas of southwestern British Columbia have been shown to subsist largely on waterfowl, especially Buffleheads and Horned Grebes (Campbell et al. 1990).

Snowy Owl

Ramiel Papish 1996

Northern Hawk-Owl
Surnia ulula

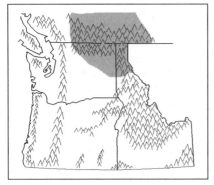

This rare northern wanderer enters the region mainly in eastern British Columbia, where it is occasional, and in the Idaho panhandle. Cannings et al. (1987) treat it as casual in the Okanagan Valley, where breeding is suspected on nearby mountains. There are at least nine winter records for Idaho, all in the panhandle. Six have reached southwestern British Columbia.

There are several winter records from Washington in addition to a few in late fall. These include one on December 21, 1914, at Pullman, two in the winter of 1919-20 along the Skagit River, December 5, 1926, at Yakima, December 1, 1959, on Grassy Top Mountain, Pend Oreille County. More recently, there was one west of Spokane in December 1992, another at Pearygin

Lake, Okanogan County, from January 24 to February 17, 1993, and one photographed on the Winthrop CBC, December 28, 1995 (which remained until January 4, 1996). Wahl (1993) notes a few additional reports from Whatcom County along Puget Sound in the northwestern corner of Washington. One bird spent much of the winter of 1996-97 on the campus of Eastern Washington University in Cheney, south of Spokane.

Oregon has reported the species twice, once at Sauvie Island during the winter of 1973-74 (accepted by Gilligan et al. 1994, but not by the OBRC) and one photographed on January 12-13, 1983, at Palmer Junction in northern Union County, and accepted by the OBRC as the first confirmed record for Oregon.

Northern Hawk-Owl

Cheney, WA
February 1997
Photograph by Ruth
Sullivan

138

Northern Pygmy-Owl
Glaucidium gnoma

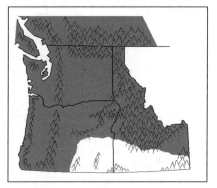

This common species winters mainly in coniferous forests, and is especially noticeable east of the Cascades, where it is easy to find along the edges of forests up to the snow line. Its abundance at higher elevations is hard to determine owing to limited access and little research. Because this species eats mainly small birds, it may move downslope when most of the semi-hardy prey species such as kinglets and chickadees do.

It is less common and local in forests at low elevations west of the Cascades, where forest habitat is more broken. West of the high Cascades this species is often found in wooded draws leading down from forested hills. It is absent from the open country of eastern Oregon and southern Idaho and is hard to find in coastal lowlands.

Location	Trend	Circles	Birds/100 ph
BC	1.6	25	0.29
WA	0.1	15	0.28
OR	0.3	38	0.19
ALL	0.5	235	0.16

Burrowing Owl
Athene cunicularia

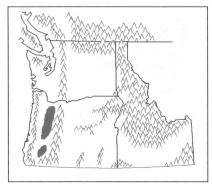

A few birds can be found in the Willamette and Rogue valleys of Oregon, with scattered records elsewhere, especially on the southern Oregon coast. The species is rare and decreasing in southwestern British Columbia, very rare east of the Cascades in British Columbia, Washington, and Oregon, and very rare in southern Idaho in winter.

Spotted Owl
Strix occidentalis

This is an uncommon, local, and declining resident of old-growth forests dominated by Douglas-fir. It is found from southwestern British Columbia (where it is rare), southward west of the Cascade summit, with a significant population in east-slope forests within the Wenatchee National Forest in Chelan, Kittitas, and Yakima counties, WA, and a small population in the east-slope forests of Klamath County, OR. It is absent from Vancouver Island, and does not occur in open country or in younger trees—therefore it is not found on the floor of the western interior valleys.

Barred Owl
Strix varia

This species' range has been expanding so rapidly that an accurate estimate of its winter occurrence is necessarily speculative. In general terms, it is uncommon to occasional in wooded areas of British Columbia, Washington, most of Oregon, and northern Idaho. Birds have been found occasionally to southern Idaho. It has reached 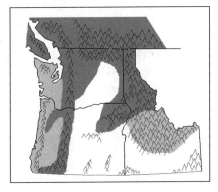 Vancouver Island and is considered relatively common as far south as the central Oregon Cascades. It is less often reported in the westernmost parts of the coast ranges and along the coast, but to what extent this results from lack of searching is not clear. This species can now be expected anywhere in the region.

Location	Trend	Circles	Birds/100 ph
BC	-0.7	14	0.12
ALL	0.7	1166	0.25

Great Gray Owl
Strix nebulosa

This owl is resident in the Rocky Mountain portion of the region, in the Wallowa and Blue mountains of Oregon, and in south-central Oregon forests. This unwary species has a strong preference for montane meadows where its preferred rodent prey is common, and therefore is generally absent from the Cascades of  Washington and northern Oregon, where such openings are rare. However, some recent records have come from the wooded edges of clear-cuts. There is some downslope movement in winter, with birds seen in open areas where they do not breed.

In Washington, Great Gray Owls occur locally in the ranges east of the Okanagan Valley, with reports coming mainly from the northeastern corner of the state and rarely in the Blue Mountains. In southern British Columbia the species is most often reported in winter from the Princeton-Merritt region west of the Okanagan. In some years a few birds descend to the Fraser lowlands. It is a vagrant to the Vancouver area, with about eight records.

It is also present in a disjunct population from the vicinity of Bend, OR, south to northern California, with most birds found in meadows with adjacent aspen and dense stands of Lodgepole Pine along the lower eastern slopes of the Cascades and in the forests of the Williamson and Sprague river drainages. Smaller numbers can be found higher in the central Cascades on both

Great Gray Owl

sides of the summit ridge in Lane and Douglas counties, OR, where the species uses both natural openings and recent clear-cuts. See Goggans and Platt (1992) for further information about this population.

In Idaho, this species is most often reported in winter from the panhandle (where it is occasional) and from the eastern part of the state (where it is uncommon to occasional). It is irregular and local in the southwestern part of the state.

Long-eared Owl
Asio otus

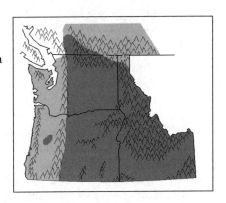

This is one of the least known owls in the region. It winters east of the Cascades throughout the region, but because it often forms large roosts in winter the actual status in a given area depends on whether the roosts are known. It is uncommon and local in southern Idaho. It is uncommon in the Okanagan Valley, BC, rare in the southwestern part of the province, and apparently absent in the Kootenay region. It appears to be most common at roosts in the wheat country of southeast Washington and northern Oregon, where a roost of fifty birds in Walla Walla County, WA, is believed to be the largest known in the region (M. Denny, personal communication).

West of the Cascades it is even less well understood, but roosts and individual birds are sometimes found. Wahl (1995) notes that the species has been found in coastal northwestern Washington and, when foraging during daylight, can be confused with Short-eared Owls. One roost has existed near Corvallis, Benton County, OR, for several years.

This species prefers very dense lowland groves for winter roosting, typically willow, Russian olive, or juniper east of the Cascades. Dense stands of ash or evergreens are favored west of the mountains.

Location	Trend	Circles	Birds/100 ph
OR	0.2	15	0.30
ALL	-1.6	709	0.11

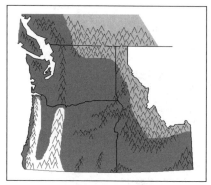

Short-eared Owl
Asio flammeus

The Short-eared Owl winters throughout the region in marshes, fields, and other open areas, generally at low elevations. Numbers vary considerably from year to year, and it tends to concentrate at favored locations, roosting on the ground or in low shrubs. Most birds leave the colder uplands east of the Cascades in winter, but some remain, especially in the Columbia-Snake river lowlands. It is occasional in the Okanagan in winter and uncommon in southwestern British Columbia, where almost all winter records in the province occur in the Fraser delta, where roosts of scores of birds can sometimes be found. Numbers in the western interior valleys and along the coast increase in winter.

A regionwide decrease in numbers is shown by CBC trend data. Since this species is relatively easy to see and count accurately when seen, this probably represents an actual decrease in the wintering population.

Location	Trend	Circles	Birds/100 ph
BC	-2.5	18	0.44
WA	-2.4	29	0.24
OR	-0.5	27	0.27
ALL	-1.8	958	0.20

Boreal Owl
Aegolius funereus

Knowledge of this species is increasing rapidly, although its habits make determining its winter status difficult. It is resident in the Rocky Mountains of Idaho and eastern British Columbia, the Wallowa and Blue mountains of Oregon, and the Cascade range south at least to the vicinity of Waldo Lake, Lane County, OR. Within this range it varies in abundance, but its true status is poorly known except where it has been well studied, as in the mountains of west-central Idaho. Although it is rarely reported in winter south of northern Idaho and eastern Washington, there is no reason to think that it does not winter in or close to its breeding range.

Away from its mountain habitat it has been reported occasionally in the lowlands. One was collected on January 10, 1974, at Pullman, Whitman County, WA (Mattocks et al. 1976). There is a specimen record from Fort Klamath, OR, from March 21, 1902 (Gabrielson and Jewett 1940) and one on January 20, 1881, noted from "the Oregon Cascades" included without further details in Gilligan et al. (1994). The Klamath basin record constitutes the southernmost record from the region at any season.

Northern Saw-whet Owl
Aegolius acadicus

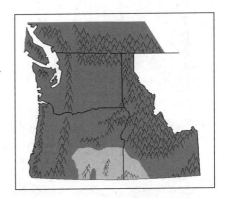

This owl winters throughout the region but is infrequently reported and not well understood. It is rare on the western part of Vancouver Island, probably because of lack of coverage. In most of the region it prefers roosting in dense stands of evergreen trees adjacent to open areas for hunting. It often uses relatively young trees, such as stands of Douglas-fir 30-40 feet high. Some birds use swampy areas with dense ash or willows or other dense riparian areas. Its relative abundance cannot be stated with any confidence, as most winter data is from CBCs, and represents the effort of a few people in a small part of the species' habitat.

Location	Trend	Circles	Birds/100 ph
BC	0.6	21	0.08
OR	0.4	30	0.05
ALL	0.3	472	0.04

Order APODIFORMES
Family Trochilidae

Black-chinned Hummingbird
Archilochus alexandri

This species does not normally winter in the region. The only records of which I am aware are of one on the Columbia Estuary CBC in 1983 (considered unacceptable by Gilligan et al. 1994), and one on December 29, 1980, on the Indian Mountain CBC in the Idaho panhandle.

Anna's Hummingbird
Calypte anna

This species has expanded its winter range into the Northwest in the past thirty years, experiencing a steady increase in range and some increase in numbers, especially at the fringes of its range. It winters widely at lower elevations west of the Cascades, especially where feeders are plentiful. On the southern Oregon coast a few birds can be found in areas far from feeders. Breeding has been confirmed as early as February in the Rogue Valley.

East of the Cascades it remains very rare, but there have been winter reports in Oregon at Bend (now an annual overwintering bird in mild years) and Camp Sherman, Jefferson County; in Washington at Wenatchee, Spokane, and Walla Walla; in Idaho at Boise and Lewiston; and rarely to the Okanagan Valley, BC.

Location	Trend	Circles	Birds/100 ph
BC	2.5	21	0.11
OR	4.9	21	0.41
ALL	3.9	226	0.75

Costa's Hummingbird
Calypte costae

One record is generally accepted in British Columbia, on December 27, 1983, in Vancouver. This bird is very rare in winter in Oregon. Two winter records have been accepted by the OBRC. A male was at Florence, Lane County, on January 31, 1980. Another male was at Newport, Lincoln County, on December 28, 1984. One was reported on the Coos Bay, OR, CBC in 1988 and one wintered in Grants Pass in 1996-97.

Rufous Hummingbird
Selasphorus rufus

There are a few winter records of this species in the region in winter, and additional records of unidentified *Selasphorus* hummingbirds. It is most often reported in southwestern Oregon. A remarkable record of a bird coming to a Victoria feeder on January 8-9, 1983, under snowy conditions speaks to the possibility of this species occurring far north as a winter lingerer (Campbell et al. 1990).

Allen's Hummingbird
Selasphorus sasin

Although there are no confirmed winter records of this species in the region, some reports of *Selasphorus* hummingbirds in winter on the southern Oregon coast may be of Allen's Hummingbird.

Order CORACIIFORMES
Family Alcedinidae
Subfamily Cerylinae

Belted Kingfisher
Ceryle alcyon

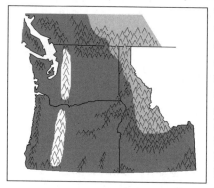

This species winters throughout the region where open fish-bearing water is available. Kingfishers can be quite common in winter along waters near the coast, and are relatively common along streams and lakes in the western interior valleys. East of the Cascades many birds depart from higher elevations and from interior British Columbia, eastern Oregon, and northern Idaho.

Location	Trend	Circles	Birds/100 ph
BC	2.1	44	0.95
ID	0.0	18	1.59
WA	1.6	35	1.75
OR	1.0	41	1.52
ALL	0.9	1791	1.07

Belted Kingfisher

Order PICIFORMES
Family Picidae
Subfamily Picinae

Lewis' Woodpecker
Melanerpes lewis

This woodpecker winters locally in Oregon and Washington, with principal concentrations in the lower Deschutes River valley and the Rogue Valley of Oregon, where it frequents oaks. It was formerly common to uncommon in winter in the southern half of the Willamette Valley, but today it is rare to occasional. It is occasional in the Umpqua Valley.

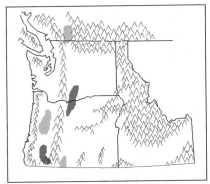

A few can be found in winter in eastern Oregon and Washington. It is uncommon in the Okanagan Valley and a vagrant to southwestern British Columbia, and rare but regular in Idaho in winter.

Some birds that winter west of the Cascades come from populations east of the mountains, moving through the Cascades in late summer, then downslope to wintering areas.

Location	Trend	Circles	Birds/100 ph
OR	-0.4	17	0.55
ALL	-1.0	199	0.56

Red-headed Woodpecker
Melanerpes erythrocephalus

There is one regional record in winter, at Nampa, ID, on December 30, 1976 (Taylor and Trost 1987).

Acorn Woodpecker
Melanerpes formicivorus

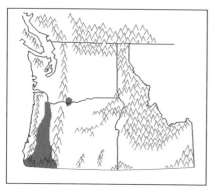

This bird is resident in western Oregon, with most birds in the Umpqua, Rogue, and southern Willamette valleys. Local populations exist at The Dalles, OR, and Lyle, WA, on opposite sides of the Columbia River gorge. A small population extends east along the Klamath River canyon into southwest Klamath County, OR. It is somewhat more common on the west side of the Willamette Valley, where there are more oaks in the rain shadow of the coast range. It becomes less frequent north to the end of its range near Banks, Washington County, OR. The species is essentially sedentary, thus winter range approximates breeding range.

Location	Trend	Circles	Birds/100 ph
OR	-0.9	16	2.13
ALL	-0.8	162	3.47

Red-bellied Woodpecker
Melanerpes carolinus

This bird is a vagrant. There is one winter record for Idaho. A bird was observed and photographed at a feeder southwest of Coeur d'Alene; it stayed from October 1992 to January 1993.

Red-bellied Woodpecker

*Coeur d'Alene, ID,
December 31, 1992
(Photograph by Dan
Svingen)*

Red-naped Sapsucker
Sphyrapicus nuchalis

Most birds leave the region by late autumn, but a few remain, primarily at lowland sites near the eastern edge of the Cascades in Oregon and locally in southern Idaho. A few winter records exist for western Washington and Oregon. There are three records for southwestern British Columbia in winter. *Note:* All winter records of

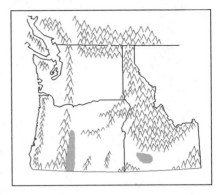

this species should be treated with caution, as they might pertain to the similar Yellow-bellied Sapsucker, whose occurrence in the western part of the region in winter is perhaps as likely.

Yellow-bellied Sapsucker
Sphyrapicus varius

This is a rare vagrant from east of the Rocky Mountains. An immature male was at Brookings, Curry County, OR, February 24-25, 1991. An immature female was at Salem in the winter of 1994-95. There is one winter record for Washington of an adult at Ellensburg, Kittitas County, from December 16, 1989 to February 18, 1990. One was in St. Maries, ID, on December 28, 1993. One male was at Shaughnessy Park, Vancouver, BC, from December 17, 1989 to March 24, 1990, and returned to the same site in the winter of 1990-91 and 1991-92.

Some winter birds are possibly misidentified as Red-naped Sapsucker (see note under previous species).

Red-breasted Sapsucker
Sphyrapicus ruber

This sapsucker winters mainly in the coast ranges and lowland western Oregon and Washington and in lowland southwestern British Columbia, with a few birds reported from the Klamath Basin and south-central Oregon. It is a winter vagrant to southeast Washington. It is uncommon in most years, but

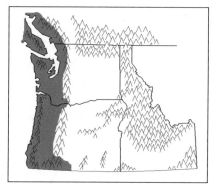

abundance in lowland valleys varies markedly from year to year depending on how many birds come how far down from the Cascades; these movements are thought to be correlated at least in part with snowfall.

Differences, if any, between wintering habits of the northern subspecies and the *daggetti* race that occurs in south-central Oregon are not clear.

Williamson's Sapsucker
Sphyrapicus thyroideus

This species winters mainly south of the region, but single birds appear fairly often in winter in lower-elevation pine stands east of the Cascades. It is rare in Idaho in winter, and there are no records to date for British Columbia.

Nuttall's Woodpecker
Picoides nuttallii

Two specimens were taken at Ashland, Jackson County, OR, on February 3-4, 1881 (*Condor* 67: 269-70, 1965). They are in the British Museum; the male is B.M. 88.10.10.7406; female 88.10.10.7407.

Downy Woodpecker
Picoides pubescens

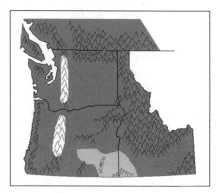

This woodpecker is common in winter west of the Cascades and in riparian areas throughout the region, with fewer birds in the colder regions east of the Cascades. Numbers do not vary widely from year to year, perhaps because the riparian areas frequented by this species are mainly at low elevations where observers concentrate, while high-elevation forests tend to be dominated by Hairy Woodpeckers and other species.

Downy Woodpecker

153

Location	Trend	Circles	Birds/100 ph
BC	0.1	44	2.33
ID	2.9	19	0.93
WA	1.3	36	1.27
OR	0.3	44	0.89

There appears to be less seasonal movement in this species than in some other smaller woodpeckers, but some birds in colder parts of the region move south or downslope.

Hairy Woodpecker
Picoides villosus

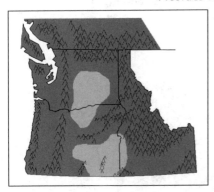

This species is uncommon in most of the region in winter, although it can be locally easy to find, especially in the coast ranges and in forests from the Cascades eastward. Numbers are generally equal to numbers of Downy Woodpeckers in the coast ranges, although Hairy Woodpeckers use more heavily timbered areas while Downy Woodpeckers tend to stay in riparian zones. In the western interior valleys this species can be hard to find in winter, and is heavily outnumbered by Downy Woodpeckers.

Location	Trend	Circles	Birds/100 ph
BC	1.5	46	1.60
ID	2.0	18	0.73
WA	-0.6	33	0.54
OR	-0.9	42	0.63
ALL	0.4	1944	1.60

White-headed Woodpecker
Picoides albolarvatus

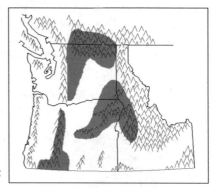

Although most field guides give the impression that this species is resident in pine forests of the Northwest, it seems that many actually leave the region in winter or become extremely hard to find. Some can be found in winter throughout the ponderosa pine-dominated areas east of the Cascades, but numbers are usually low and the species is often unreported. It does occur north to the Okanagan Valley in winter.

This "fading away" during winter may be partly an artifact of a substantial drop in observer coverage of pine forests during winter or of the tendency of males to forage higher than females in winter (as noted in Ehrlich et al. 1988), but some CBCs cover significant tracts of pine forest and report very few birds, and forays into this habitat later in winter do not have much better success. It seems likely that a portion of the population leaves the region in winter.

Three-toed Woodpecker
Picoides tridactylus

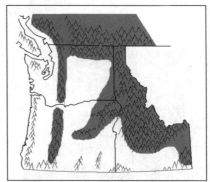

Winter status for this species is difficult to determine owing to the almost complete absence of observer coverage of snow-covered habitat during winter. A few birds appear at downslope locations, but data are insufficient to reach any conclusions regarding these movements.

The winter range is probably essentially the same as the breeding range, including lodgepole pine and fir forests, mainly above 4,000 feet, in the

Cascades from Mt. McLoughlin, OR, north through British Columbia, and in the Rockies and attached ranges south locally to the southern Blue and Ochoco mountains of Oregon. Winter status in southern Lake County, OR, is unknown.

This species is very rare in Vancouver Island and southwestern British Columbia in winter.

Black-backed Woodpecker
Picoides arcticus

There are more records of this species in winter than of Three-toed Woodpecker in most of the region, but most birds seem to remain in or close to the breeding range. Fires near Bend, OR, brought several into the fringe of the pine zone in the early 1990s, and birds have occasionally been reported west of the Cascade summit as low as 2,000 feet.

This species is reported in winter in southeastern British Columbia, but unlike the Three-toed Woodpecker it does not appear in winter in the coastal mountains there or in northwestern Washington.

Northern Flicker
Colaptes auratus

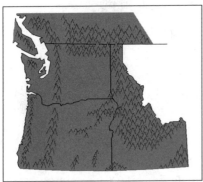

Late fall brings large movements of this species through the inland part of the region, and many of these probably end up in lowland western Oregon and Washington, where they can be locally common in winter. Many birds remain east of the Cascades, especially in towns and riparian areas where

Location	Trend	Circles	Birds/100 ph
BC	-2.8	46	4.36
ID	-0.9	18	9.09
WA	-1.2	36	9.75
OR	-0.4	45	8.21
ALL	-1.2	1900	5.00

large trees are available. Most leave high-elevation forests in winter.

"Yellow-shafted" Flickers often appear during this fall and early winter period, especially on the coast where birds sometimes concentrate, probably representing a small movement from the northern Rocky Mountains, where that form breeds east of the summit ridges.

A slight regionwide decrease is shown by CBC population trend data.

Pileated Woodpecker
Dryocopus pileatus

This resident is uncommon but widespread in winter in forested areas, and occasional locally in cities adjacent to forests, where enough large trees are available. It is absent from open areas of eastern Oregon and Washington and southern Idaho. Distribution is somewhat patchy owing to patterns of timber harvest and regrowth. It is less 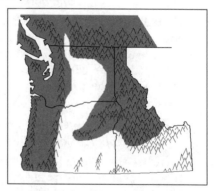 common at any season in high-elevation pine, spruce, and true fir forests, thus there is little downslope or seasonal movement in winter; however, some birds move into riparian areas and cities east of the Cascades in winter.

Location	Trend	Circles	Birds/100 ph
BC	1.1	40	0.75
WA	-0.2	27	0.17
OR	-0.8	27	0.17
ALL	1.3	1309	0.84

Order PASSERIFORMES
Family Tyrannidae
Subfamily Fluvicolinae

Least Flycatcher
Empidonax minimus

The only winter record for the region is of a bird caught, photographed, and banded near Tillamook, OR, in December, 1992. This bird was present from December 20 to 28.

Least Flycatcher

Tillamook, OR,
December 28, 1992
(Photograph by Craig Roberts)

Hammond's Flycatcher
Empidonax hammondii

The only generally accepted winter record for the region is of a bird observed on the Roseburg, OR, CBC in 1992 (a description is on file with the regional CBC editor). A bird at Blue Creek, Walla Walla, WA, CBC on December 16, 1990, is considered not acceptable by the WBRC.

Pacific-slope/Cordilleran: "Western" Flycatcher
Empidonax difficilis/occidentalis complex

There have been several reports for the region in winter, but the only one generally accepted was on the Grants Pass, OR, CBC in 1993. Good drawings and a description have been provided for this bird, which was seen by an experienced observer.

Eastern Phoebe
Sayornis phoebe

The only winter records from the region are of single birds December 16 and 23, 1989, at Bay Center, Pacific County, WA (see Paulson and Mattocks 1992) and February 19-20, 1996, at Independence, Polk County, OR. This eastern species is a vagrant to the region and can appear at any season.

Black Phoebe
Sayornis nigricans

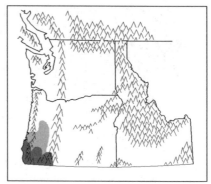

This species is more common in southwestern Oregon than it was twenty years ago. It is locally common to uncommon on the southern Oregon coast to the Coquille Valley, especially around the towns of Coquille and Myrtle Point, where the CBC finds one hundred or more birds. Numbers are still increasing in these areas in the 1990s. It is also locally common to uncommon in the Rogue Valley north to northern Josephine County. In recent years more birds have been seen in west-central Oregon and east to the Klamath Basin, but the species is still rare in these areas.

Elsewhere in the region, the species is a rare vagrant but it has been reported more often in western Oregon in the 1990s. There is one winter record at Moclips, Grays Harbor County, WA, on February 27, 1980.

Say's Phoebe
Sayornis saya

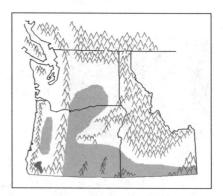

This semi-hardy flycatcher is uncommon to occasional in winter in the eastern Rogue Valley, and occasional to rare elsewhere in southwestern Oregon. East of the Cascades it is rare but regular in lowland areas of southern Idaho, eastern Oregon, and southeastern Washington, with single birds occurring every few years, especially in the basins of south-central Oregon and along the Columbia and Snake rivers. It is rare in northwestern Oregon, western Washington, and British Columbia.

This is one of the earliest spring migrants to arrive in the region, frequently appearing in Oregon, southern Idaho, and the Okanagan Valley by late February.

Vermilion Flycatcher

Ridgefield, WA
Photograph by Ruth
Sullivan

Vermilion Flycatcher
Pyrocephalus rubinus

This species is a vagrant from the southwestern United States. An adult male was at Myrtle Point, Coos County, OR, on December 6-7, 1992; this record has been accepted by the OBRC. An adult male was near Redmond, King County, WA, on January 25, 1988, and remained until March (Tweit and Skriletz 1996). A female was at Ridgefield NWR near Vancouver, WA, in December-January 1995-96, where it was seen by many observers.

Subfamily Tyranninae

Ash-throated Flycatcher
Myiarchus cinerascens

There are a few winter reports in the region. The Dusky-capped Flycatcher is almost as likely in winter.

Dusky-capped Flycatcher

Newport, OR, January 1996
Photograph by Tim Janzen

Dusky-capped Flycatcher
Myiarchus tuberculifer

This is a vagrant. The only record for the region spent most of January 1996 in Newport, OR.

Tropical Kingbird
Tyrannus melancholicus

This species moves up the west coast in small numbers after the breeding season, and a few birds reach the Northwest in most autumns. Most of these disappear by December, but there are a few winter records for the region.

Western Kingbird
Tyrannus verticalis

Despite a number of CBC reports, I am aware of no verified winter record of this species in the Northwest in winter.

Family Laniidae
Subfamily Laniidae

Northern Shrike
Lanius excubitor

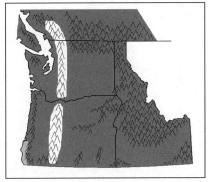

This species is the "winter shrike" that replaces the Loggerhead Shrike in most of the region between late October and mid-April. It arrives in southern British Columbia by mid-October (Cannings et al.,1989) and in the southern part of the region by late in the month.

Although abundance varies somewhat from year to year, the species is usually uncommon in open country with available perches throughout the region east of the Cascades, in the Willamette Valley, and locally in the coastal region of British Columbia, Washington, and northern Oregon. It is somewhat less regular in numbers in the Rogue and Umpqua valleys but is usually present, especially in the Rogue Valley. It is also less regular in the Klamath Basin.

Grays Harbor, WA, averages 5.8 birds per CBC, Tillamook Bay on the northern Oregon coast averages 2.2 birds per count, while Coos Bay, OR, on the south coast, an area with considerable habitat for the species, finds an average one bird each year and often misses the species completely.

Location	Trend	Circles	Birds/100 ph
BC	-0.1	38	0.53
ID	-1.1	18	0.79
WA	-0.2	34	1.09
OR	1.8	42	1.32
ALL	0.2	1102	0.42

Oregon shows a slight increase in CBC tallies over time while the rest of the region shows a slight decrease. This may represent a tendency of birds in recent years to go farther south and west in winter. Unusual movements of birds south into New England in the mid-1990s may reflect a similar trend on the other side of the continent.

Loggerhead Shrike
Lanius ludovicianus

Although most Loggerhead Shrikes leave the region in winter, some remain east of the Cascades in lowland areas or even at relatively high elevations (4,100 feet at Malheur NWR, OR) where sufficient prey is available. They are rare north to the Okanagan Valley and the Vancouver area in British Columbia in winter.

The species is most regular in winter in the Klamath Basin, the Columbia River bottoms east to the Tri-Cities, WA, area, at Malheur NWR, and at lowland locales in eastern Oregon and southern Idaho. It is annual in small numbers in most of these areas. It is nearly annual in the Rogue Valley in winter, and there are a few winter records elsewhere west of the Cascades in Oregon, mainly in the southwestern part of the state, including the coast. There is at least one winter record from Vancouver, BC. At all locations the Northern Shrike is the most common species present in winter, but as more observers are in the field east of the Cascades in winter it has become apparent that the Loggerhead Shrike remains to winter more often and in greater numbers than previously known. Whether this represents a change in distribution of birds or of observers is not clear.

Location	Trend	Circles	Birds/100 ph
OR	1.5	27	0.23
WA	-4.2	14	0.15
ALL	-1.7	1183	2.00

Northern Shrikes typically prefer to hunt where there is more tree and shrub cover than do Loggerhead Shrikes, which are more common in open sagebrush.

Family Vireonidae
Subfamily Vireoninae

Hutton's Vireo
Vireo huttoni

This is the only resident vireo in the region; it is uncommon west of the high Cascades throughout the region, especially where deciduous trees are mixed with conifers. It is not common anywhere but can be found fairly easily in the right habitat, where it often flocks in winter with kinglets and chickadees.

Hutton's Vireos are most common in southwestern Oregon and in the coastal ranges and lowland forests. They are much less regular in the Cascades above the foothills. A small number of birds occur east of the Cascades in the complex mixed forests in southwestern Klamath County, OR. The species is rare to occasional in southwestern British Columbia in winter.

Location	Trend	Circles	Birds/100 ph
BC	1.2	15	0.12
OR	0.5	24	0.27
WA	2.6	21	0.12
ALL	2.1	190	0.23

Family Corvidae

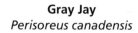

Gray Jay
Perisoreus canadensis

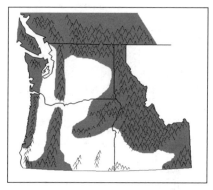

This jay is common in all of the forested mountainous parts of the region, mainly above 3,000 feet, except in coastal areas. This resident jay, bane of summer campers, provides a quiet accent to the apparently birdless montane regions in winter. It can be found above the snow line in forested mountains throughout the region, and locally to sea level in the coast ranges.

Although very few CBCs are held in this species' primary concentration areas, it appears that it is common to uncommon in most of its habitat, with local gaps in the Oregon coast range, especially in Coos County, where there is little available habitat. In the Cascades and Rocky Mountains these birds sometimes come down to lower elevations in winter, but most seem to remain in the snow zone.

Location	Trend	Circles	Birds/100 ph
BC	0.0	30	1.80
OR	-0.1	23	0.31
ALL	2.2	382	1.46

Steller's Jay
Cyanocitta stelleri

This species is abundant to uncommon throughout the region in coniferous forests. It has expanded its habitat usage in the past twenty years and is now more common in towns and cities away from conifers. This may be the change that is reflected in CBC trend data, which show an increase in the wintering population. The

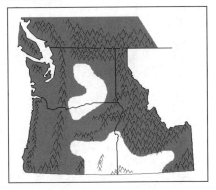

species remains common in the mountains in winter, but some birds move downslope, resulting in some buildup in lowland fringes and movement into cities.

Location	Trend	Circles	Birds/100 ph
BC	4.1	46	5.08
WA	1.3	33	3.83
OR	2.2	42	4.19
ALL	0.5	374	3.34

Steller's Jay

Blue Jay
Cyanocitta cristata

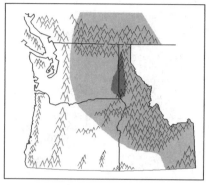

This rare to occasional visitor from east of the Rocky Mountains has become more regular in the region in the past twenty years, with invasion years bringing scores of birds and even "off years" providing a few. Although single birds reach the western interior valleys, Puget Sound, and even the outer coast in years of major movement, the principal wintering area for these birds in the region is eastern Washington, northeastern Oregon, most of Idaho, and the interior valleys of southern British Columbia. In this area the species is occasional, with flocks of two or three birds sometimes present in peak years. Even in invasion years this species rarely reaches southwestern Oregon, and often fails to reach the coast. It is a vagrant to the Vancouver area, BC, with about eight fall and winter records.

Western Scrub-Jay
Aphelocoma californica

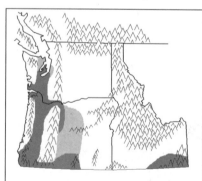

The Western Scrub-Jay is abundant in the western interior valleys of Oregon and less common and more local north to southern Puget Sound, the mouth of the Columbia River, the Columbia River gorge, and along the southern border of Oregon. It is locally uncommon in southeastern Idaho. This species has been expanding in the past twenty years, and its range is now somewhat complex. It remains abundant in the western interior valleys and foothills of Oregon and north to the area around Kelso, WA. Farther north it diminishes somewhat in numbers

Location	Trend	Circles	Birds/100 ph
OR	2.4	24	5.66
ALL	1.0	354	5.18

(probably because of the decrease in oaks) until its range fades out along the southern shores of Puget Sound. In recent years birds have been reported more often farther north along the sound to Seattle and the islands. The species is a vagrant to British Columbia. One stayed at Musqueam Park, Vancouver, from July 1993 through April 1994.

On the coast the species has historically been present in Curry County, OR, from Nesika Beach south to California. This population does not seem to be spreading, although birds appear from time to time farther north on the coast. In Coos County, OR, the species sometimes moves in winter as far west as Coquille. The major expansion on the coast has been down the Columbia River to Astoria, OR, where this bird now breeds and is resident. Many pairs are now present in this area.

East of the Cascades, Scrub-Jays occur locally east to The Dalles, OR, and Lyle, WA, and in the northern Deschutes River canyon. In the early 1990s a population in Bend, Deschutes County, OR, has increased to at least twenty-five birds. Birds have been found elsewhere in central and eastern Oregon with increasing frequency. They also occur in southern Klamath County and southern Lake County around Adel. This latter population (along with birds in Idaho) probably represents "Woodhouse's Jay," the distinct Great Basin subspecies occasionally considered for full species status.

Because of the species' expansion in eastern Oregon, wanderers could be from either the westside population or from the Great Basin population.

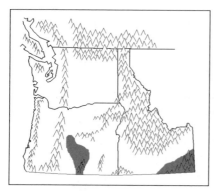

Pinyon Jay
*Gymnorhinus
cyanocephalus*

This species is abundant but very local in central and south-central Oregon and in southeastern Idaho. It forms large flocks in fall and winter in the juniper zone, so it is typically found by the score—or the hundred—or not at all. Birds are sometimes found outside the species' normal range, but not very often compared to other corvids.

Clark's Nutcracker
Nucifraga columbiana

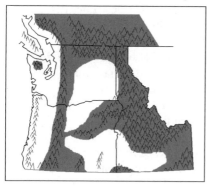

This species is common in the high Cascades, Olympics, Rocky Mountains, and ancillary ranges in winter, but is usually absent from the coast ranges. It is also common in the Okanagan Valley in winter, but is less often found in valley areas farther south. Owing to its montane habits its relative abundance is not well known. It sometimes comes downslope in small numbers, especially into junipers east of the Cascades. In rare years small invasions occur, pushing birds into the lowlands, the western interior valleys, and even to the coast.

Location	Trend	Circles	Birds/100 ph
BC	4.1	15	1.51
OR	-0.5	15	1.02
ALL	2.1	196	1.54

Black-billed Magpie
Pica pica

This is one of the most common and widespread birds east of the Cascades, and is most abundant in the Columbia-Snake river lowlands, the Okanagan Valley, and other agricultural areas, especially where there are plenty of small trees nearby. It also occurs to relatively high elevations in small mountain valleys in the Blue and Rocky mountains.

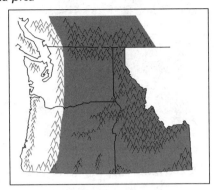

It is rare west of the Cascades, with most records coming from the Rogue Valley and the east side of the Willamette Valley, plus several from northern Puget Sound. The Medford, OR, CBC records the species about one year out of five; it is much more rare elsewhere west of the Cascades. One was at Burnaby, BC, on January 14, 1994.

Location	Trend	Circles	Birds/100 ph
BC	-2.9	19	6.23
ID	-1.8	18	92.83
WA	2.2	14	18.63
OR	-3.5	24	29.17
ALL	-1.3	366	21.11

American Crow
Corvus brachyrhynchos

Northwestern Crow
Corvus caurinus

These birds are abundant in most of the region except for montane forest, desert, and rimrock areas. The conventional wisdom is that American Crows occur north to southwestern Washington on the coast and to central inland British Columbia, while Northwestern Crows are the sole coastal crow from Puget Sound north to Alaska. Because of doubts regarding the status of the Northwestern Crow as a species and the lack of

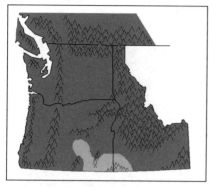

agreement on where the ranges change, they are treated together here.

In Washington the American Crow is thought to be increasing while the Northwestern Crow is decreasing, but this probably reflects changes in observers' reporting patterns, especially the tendency to treat small crows as "crow, sp." for CBC and other purposes (Phil Mattocks, personal communication).

There have been reports of "Northwestern" Crows south to the northern Oregon coast. Today most CBC compilers in the overlap zone treat crows as either American (the usual practice in Oregon) or "crow, sp." (the most common practice in Puget Sound). Contrary to Root (1988), "Northwestern" Crows do *not* occur "in the mountains along the Pacific Coast from slightly north of Eugene, Oregon."

In the colder parts of the region, crows often form large winter roosts containing hundreds or even thousands of birds.

Northwestern Crow

Location	Trend	Circles	Birds/100 ph
WA	-9.5	17	21.73
BC	2.4	31	136.24
ALL	2.5	53	65.70

American Crow

Location	Trend	Circles	Birds/100 ph
BC	-1.6	22	32.57
ID	-3.5	19	43.71
WA	13.5	28	29.66
OR	2.1	40	26.69
ALL	1.9	1924	65.52

Common Raven
Corvus corax

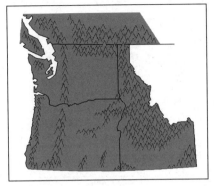

The Common Raven is abundant to uncommon in most of the region except in urban areas. This large corvid replaces the crows in montane areas, desert, and rimrock areas. It is thus most common from the Cascade range eastward, but it can also be quite common in the coast ranges. It occurs as a common to uncommon visitor in the western interior valleys and on the outer coast. Ravens are least common in the northern Willamette Valley. On the southern Oregon coast they can be as common as are crows in some areas, feeding on the beaches much as crows do. The species is uncommon in the lowlands of eastern Idaho.

The wintering population throughout the region is generally expanding, according to CBC trend data. Ravens are doing well in their traditional haunts and have also been noted more often in urban areas in recent years.

Location	Trend	Circles	Birds/100 ph
BC	2.4	48	35.71
ID	5.0	19	6.47
WA	7.4	27	4.41
OR	4.4	44	8.93
ALL	3.5	877	16.89

Family Alaudidae

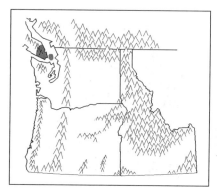

Sky Lark
Alauda arvensis

This is an introduced resident at Saanich, southern Vancouver Island, and small numbers winter on the island around Martindale Flats. It has also been present on San Juan Island, WA, since 1960.

Horned Lark
Eremophila alpestris

The Horned Lark is abundant to uncommon east of the Cascades in open country, local and uncommon to occasional west of the Cascades. This species forms large flocks in open areas east of the Cascades, with numbers sometimes reaching the hundreds in a single flock. It is most common in areas of open sagebrush, short grass, open dirt, gravel, mudflat, and sometimes alkali pans. West of the Cascades it is much less common and more local, with small resident populations at the mouth of the Columbia River and in the central Willamette Valley.

Location	Trend	Circles	Birds/100 ph
ID	0.1	15	42.40
WA	-3.9	17	36.46
OR	3.6	32	11.12
ALL	-0.5	1632	81.80

Family Hirundinidae
Subfamily Hirundininae

Tree Swallow
Tachycineta bicolor

This swallow is rare but regular in southwestern Oregon in winter, with most records in the western interior valleys. It is rare farther north, and absent east of the Cascades. Tree Swallows are among the last birds to leave the more temperate parts of the region, and a few remain in most years at least into mid-December.

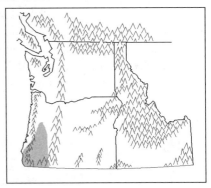

The species is most often reported from Eugene south to Medford, OR, with multiple birds present in some years. There are records north to western Washington and British Columbia, but the species is not annual in these areas.

There are very few winter reports for coastal areas, despite the attractiveness of the coast for lingering birds of many families. It is not clear why this is true, but the more limited number of observers may be a factor.

This species returns to southern Oregon in mid-February and can be found in small numbers in most of the region by the end of the month.

Violet-green Swallow
Tachycineta thalassina

This bird is rare in winter, with scattered records west of the Cascades. It is not annual in any part of the region. The spring migration in Oregon begins in late January/early February, and small numbers return to the Okanagan Valley, BC, in mid-February in some years.

Cliff Swallow
Petrochelidon pyrrhonota

This bird is a rare lingerer. One was at Reifel Refuge, Ladner, BC, from December 7 to 10, 1989, for the first winter record in the province. Two birds were on Iona Island, BC, from December 7 to 11, 1991. One was at Bellingham, WA, on the 1973 CBC, the only CBC record for the state during the thirty-year data period. There are no Oregon CBC records.

Barn Swallow
Hirundo rustica

This swallow is rare in winter, but one or two seem to linger into mid-December in the region west of the Cascades and in most years. Along with the Tree Swallow, this is the most likely swallow to be found in winter.

Family Paridae

Black-capped Chickadee
Poecile atricapillus

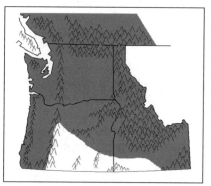

This is the common lowland chickadee found in most of the region. It is most common in deciduous and mixed woodlands in towns, riparian zones, and in other settings where deciduous trees are available. It is not usually present in montane aspen stands, ceding such areas to the Mountain Chickadee, or in pure moist coniferous forests dominated by Chestnut-backed Chickadees.

Numbers can be very high west of the Cascades, witness the 1,036 birds on the Eugene, OR, CBC in 1980 or the 617 at Olympia, WA, in 1989. East of the mountains numbers are usually lower and the species is more local, but where habitat is

Location	Trend	Circles	Birds/100 ph
BC	1.3	34	27.56
ID	4.7	18	16.17
WA	3.0	32	16.68
OR	1.4	41	7.89
ALL	2.9	1415	21.59

available significant numbers can be found, e.g. the 168 at Coeur d'Alene, ID, in 1991 or the 261 at Ellensburg, WA, in 1989. At Penticton, BC, the mean count is 142, with a record high of 361.

It is much less common in some areas, notably southeastern Oregon and the San Juan Islands, WA, and it is absent from Vancouver Island.

Numbers are increasing throughout the region according to CBC trend data.

Mountain Chickadee
Poecile gambeli

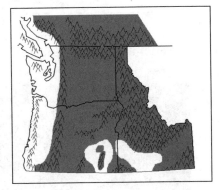

This is the common resident pine-country chickadee, and most birds remain in the ponderosa and lodgepole pine forests year-round. It also occurs in true fir. This species is also common in high-elevation aspen forests in summer, but most birds probably leave those areas in winter. Because of snow levels there are few data available from high elevations in winter.

In some years this species moves downslope in large numbers, mainly on the east side of the Cascades, with some using juniper stands. Areas that have three or four birds on a CBC one year may have two hundred the next year. A few birds appear in lowland areas west of the Cascades in most years, but major invasions on the west side are rare, happening only every ten years or so.

A general regional increase is offset by a decrease in Washington, according to CBC trend data.

Location	Trend	Circles	Birds/100 ph
ID	2.7	19	1.92
BC	5.9	27	5.40
WA	-1.1	20	2.08
OR	1.2	40	11.10
ALL	1.9	365	5.12

Chestnut-backed Chickadee
Poecile rufescens

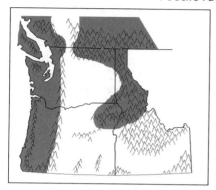

This species is abundant west of the Cascade summit and common to uncommon east of the Cascades in northern Washington, northern Idaho, and the eastern Blue Mountains of southeastern Washington and northeastern Oregon. It is locally uncommon in south-central British Columbia, especially in the West Kootenays. It is the only chickadee found on Vancouver Island.

This is the common resident chickadee of moist coniferous forests. It can be found in almost any grove of Douglas-fir west

Chestnut-backed Chickadees

Location	Trend	Circles	Birds/100 ph
BC	1.1	41	9.41
OR	1.4	31	7.88
WA	3.0	31	4.87
ALL	1.7	170	6.00

of the Cascade summit, and also occurs in spruce, hemlock, and other evergreens that occur in moist areas. It is generally absent from drier pine-dominated forests.

Some winters bring birds to the towns adjacent to the Blue Mountains. Small numbers can also be found on the west side of the Klamath Basin where the complex forest type supports several "west-side" species.

CBC trend data show that this, like the other parids, is generally increasing throughout its range in the region.

Boreal Chickadee
Poecile hudsonicus

This chickadee is uncommon and local in southeastern British Columbia and southward locally in mountainous areas to northeastern Washington and to Boundary County and Bonner County, ID. It is also resident south in the Cascades to Whatcom and Okanogan counties, WA (*Washington Breeding Bird*

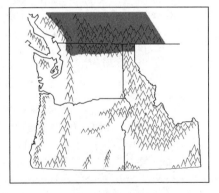

Atlas, in press 1997; visit the Washington Boreal Chickadee web page at http://salmo.cqs.washington.edu:80/~wagap/birds/pahu.gif for an update). Winter distribution is not well known owing mainly to the difficulty of access to the habitat in winter.

Juniper Titmouse
Baeolophus ridgwayi

Oak Titmouse
Baeolophus inornatus

West of line: Oak Titmouse
East of line: Juniper Titmouse

These birds of open dry woodlands enter the region only along the southern edge, where they are common in the inland Rogue Valley, along the southern edge of the Klamath Basin, and locally east to southern Idaho, where they are locally common in the southeastern part of the state.

Most birds are found in ceanothus stands, juniper and oak groves, and mountain mahogany patches, and in areas where these habitats intermingle, such as in south-central Oregon. These species are rather local, found where tendrils of preferred habitat extend into the region from the south. In addition to the Rogue Valley, birds are found in Oregon mainly in the southern Klamath Basin, the southern Warner Valley, and adjacent southern slopes of Hart Mountain. Juniper groves are the preferred habitat in southeastern Idaho.

The "Plain Titmouse" was split into these two species by AOU action in July 1997. The Oak Titmouse is the Rogue Valley species; the Juniper Titmouse occurs east of the Cascades locally to Idaho. It is not clear which species occurs in south-central Klamath County, OR.

Family Aegithalidae

Bushtit
Psaltriparus minimus

The Bushtit is abundant to uncommon west of the Cascades and locally common to uncommon in most of central and eastern Oregon, central Washington, and southern Idaho. This is one of the most common residents of open brushy areas west of the Cascades, where it occurs north to southwestern British

Columbia. CBCs typically find the species in the hundreds in urban areas and the western interior valleys, and it is common, although more local, on the outer coast. On the northern Oregon coast and the outer coast of Washington and British Columbia this species is local and can be abundant in some areas and difficult to find in others.

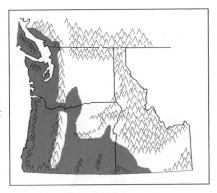

This species has been expanding its range northward and east of the Cascades in recent years. CBC numbers in western British Columbia have doubled in the past decade. Today it occurs from the juniper zone of central Oregon north to central Washington, where the Ellensburg-Yakima area represents the northern edge of its range east of the Cascades. CBC trend data reflect an increase in Washington. It also occurs in south-central Oregon and southern Idaho, where it can be found north to northern Baker County, OR, and Washington County, ID. A wintering population in southeastern Idaho disappeared during several harsh winters in the 1980s and has not recovered. It is absent from northeastern Oregon, northern Idaho, far eastern Washington, and inland British Columbia. There are two winter records in the Okanagan Valley.

Location	Trend	Circles	Birds/100 ph
WA	4.5	27	9.73
OR	0.8	35	9.67
ALL	2.7	349	7.30

Bushtits

Family Sittidae
Subfamily Sittinae

Red-breasted Nuthatch
Sitta canadensis

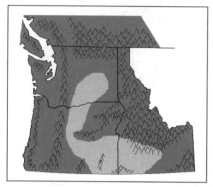

This is the most widespread nuthatch in the region in winter, occurring from the mountains to sea level where conifers are available. In most years there is a significant migratory movement downslope that brings hundreds of birds to the western interior valleys and into towns east of the Cascades. When food supplies permit, this species remains abundant in the Cascades in winter.

There is some long-distance movement as well. Birds usually reach the Snake River lowlands and other wooded areas between the Cascades and the Rockies. In most years birds reach the coast as well, but in some years the species is quite scarce that far west. It is absent from one-third to one-half of outer coast CBCs in Oregon and Washington.

Away from stands of conifers this species is much harder to find in winter, but a few remain in deciduous woodlands in lowlands east of the Cascades.

CBC trend data show a solid increase throughout the region.

Location	Trend	Circles	Birds/100 ph
BC	3.8	41	3.21
ID	5.1	14	4.36
WA	2.8	34	3.51
OR	0.9	40	3.70
ALL	2.3	1761	1.61

White-breasted Nuthatch
Sitta carolinensis

This species is common to uncommon in inland western Oregon and in forested areas east of the Cascades throughout the region. It occurs in two principal habitat types in the region in winter—oak groves and ponderosa pine forest—producing a broad distribution with some sizable areas of absence.

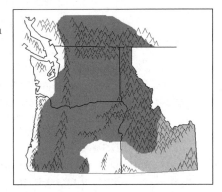

The greatest concentrations of birds west of the Cascades are in the drier oak woodlands of southwestern Oregon in the Umpqua and Rogue valleys, but the species is also common locally north through the western interior valleys to the Columbia River. Although the species is fairly common in the Portland-Sauvie Island area, numbers drop dramatically in southwestern Washington where lowland oak groves become scarce: the species is missed more often than it is found at the next CBC 40 miles north of Sauvie Island, Cowlitz-Columbia in the Longview-Kelso area.

White-breasted Nuthatch

Location	Trend	Circles	Birds/100 ph
BC	2.5	14	0.66
OR	-0.8	36	0.54
WA	-1.3	19	0.34
ALL	1.6	1749	3.02

East of the high Cascades the species is fairly common wherever there are stands of ponderosa pine, resulting in a range covering most of the forested areas east of the mountains. Like the Red-breasted Nuthatch it is somewhat irruptive, with numbers at lowland sites varying markedly from year to year. It is uncommon to occasional in southeastern Washington, southern Idaho, and far-eastern Oregon in winter. Some birds come into towns and winter at feeders or in parks.

This species is rare on the outer coast throughout the region, and is very rare in Puget Sound. Even on the southern Oregon coast where there are stands of oaks, it is very rare at any season.

Pygmy Nuthatch
Sitta pygmaea

This pine-country nuthatch is much less likely to move out of its breeding grounds in winter than either of the other nuthatches, so even CBCs located adjacent to major ponderosa pine forests typically do not find large numbers. Only counts that lie within the species' breeding zone, such as Penticton, BC, Spokane, WA, Coeur d'Alene, ID, or Bend, OR, typically find large numbers.

Location	Trend	Circles	Birds/100 ph
OR	3.2	15	1.75
ALL	0.8	184	5.10

It is very rare west of the Cascades, the only slight concentration being a few records in southwestern Oregon. Because small numbers probably breed in the Siskiyou Mountains along the southern side of the Rogue Valley, some of these west-side lowland records may represent downslope movement of a small local population.

Family Certhiidae
Subfamily Certhiinae

Brown Creeper
Certhia americana

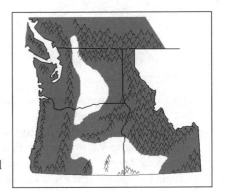

This species winters throughout the region in forested areas, and shows some downslope movement in winter. It occurs in most forest types in winter, but is most common in old-growth conifers. Numbers at lowland sites vary somewhat from year to year.

Location	Trend	Circles	Birds/100 ph
BC	0.6	46	0.69
ID	0.6	16	0.36
WA	1.1	33	0.51
OR	0.2	41	0.61
ALL	0.6	1851	0.74

Family Troglodytidae

Rock Wren
Salpinctes obsoletus

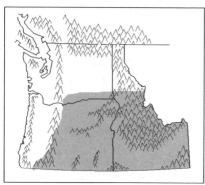

This species occurs east of the Cascades in canyons, talus slopes, and other rocky areas. Many birds leave in winter, but some remain. The size of wintering populations varies depending on the severity of the season. Some birds winter north to montane Idaho and southern British Columbia in mild winters. In most years this species can be found north to northern Oregon and southeastern Washington in small numbers. There are a few records west of the Cascades, mainly in southwestern Oregon, where it is uncommon in the eastern Rogue Valley and occurs on about one count in three at Medford. Most birds depart from eastern Washington and Idaho in winter, with a few remaining at low elevations.

Canyon Wren
Catherpes mexicanus

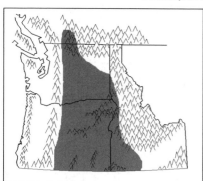

This species' range is similar to that of the Rock Wren but is more limited to large, steep-sided canyons and adjacent boulder fields. It remains in the breeding range in winter in most of our area, although birds seem to withdraw from northern Idaho. Populations decline after severe winters.

Cannings et al. (1987) note that in the southern Okanagan Valley, where the species reaches the northern end of its range, "numbers of Canyon Wrens have varied considerably from decade to decade. Apparently the species . . . is abnormally sensitive to low temperatures." Dick

Location	Trend	Circles	Birds/100 ph
OR	2.7	15	0.66
ALL	0.3	251	0.70

Cannings (personal communication) also notes that young Canyon Wrens often move north in early winter, withdrawing or not surviving when colder weather arrives. The same phenomenon has been noted by Bob Kindschy at high-elevation sites in southeastern Oregon (Contreras and Kindschy 1996).

There are not very many CBCs located in the heart of Canyon Wren country, the canyons and cliffs of the Great Basin and the Columbia-Snake tributaries.

Bewick's Wren
Thryomanes bewickii

This species is common in the western interior valleys, on the coast, and in lowland areas along Puget Sound and in southwestern British Columbia. It is locally common and expanding east of the Cascades, and is now found annually in southeast Washington and northern Idaho.

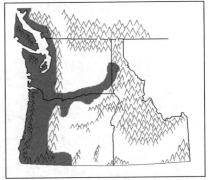

This familiar species is easy to find in brushy areas west of the Cascades, and has occurred for decades in the southern Klamath Basin and the Warner Valley of south-central Oregon. In the past thirty years it has expanded rapidly eastward and northward east of the Cascades. Today it can be found along the Columbia River east to southeastern Washington (common at the Walla Walla River mouth) and locally to northern Idaho. It has also been reported

Location	Trend	Circles	Birds/100 ph
BC	-1.3	22	2.14
WA	2.9	31	2.02
OR	1.0	31	1.85
ALL	0.6	618	1.36

Count	1968-72 average	1985-89 average	1990-94 average
Umatilla County, OR	NA	11.8	24.8
Tri-Cities, WA	2.6	13.2	12.2

with increasing frequency in central and southeastern Oregon, mainly in fall, perhaps as a post-breeding dispersal. The increase of 2.9 percent in Washington is perhaps driven by this expansion into the eastern part of the state.

This expansion can also be seen in the change in CBC records at four counts in the expansion zone. At Spokane, WA, the species was first reported in 1991, and has been annual in very small numbers since then. At Moscow, ID, it was first reported in 1989 and has been seen on two of five counts since then. It has become quite common in the Columbia lowlands and adjacent tributaries, as shown by the table above.

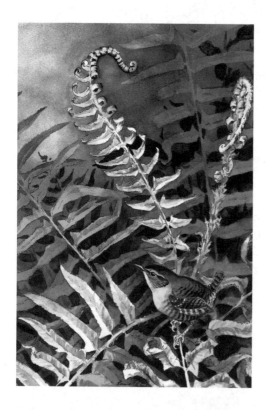

Winter Wren

House Wren
Troglodytes aedon

This species is rare in winter in the region. Almost all birds leave by late September, but a few stragglers may remain, mainly in the warmer parts of the region. There are many CBC reports of this species, but most are probably in error, representing misidentified Winter Wrens or, perhaps a greater problem, Marsh Wrens. The species should be treated as extralimital anywhere in the region in winter, and reports should be accompanied by supporting documentation.

Mike Denny (personal communication) notes that both of the generally accepted records for southeastern Washington were wintering in heated stock sheds.

One was in the central Okanagan Valley, BC, on February 16, 1995.

Winter Wren
Troglodytes troglodytes

Although some field guides indicate that the Winter Wren remains throughout the region in winter, most birds leave the colder higher elevations, and the bulk of the winter population lies west of the high Cascades in woodlands, riparian areas, urban parks, and other settings with dense undergrowth. The species also winters in small numbers to at least 3,000 feet in the western Cascades when conditions permit.

Single birds to fewer than ten is a normal count even at lowland locations east of the Cascades, and at higher elevations the species is occasional to absent. On the west side the species is locally abundant, with counts in the scores to low hundreds common at well-covered circles. The species is especially common on the coast, where the dense undergrowth it prefers is widespread.

Location	Trend	Circles	Birds/100 ph
BC	0.8	43	2.67
WA	2.9	35	2.47
OR	-0.3	40	2.76
ALL	0.6	1350	0.50

Marsh Wren
Cistothorus palustris

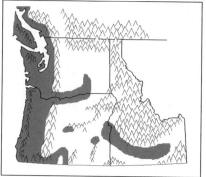

This species is generally common and can be locally abundant west of the Cascades in winter, using not only marshes but also wet fields and dense dune grass along the coast. At preferred sites, dozens of birds can be found when habitat is carefully checked. Because of its habitat preferences it is absent from large swathes of the region, but even a small marsh or wet swale with tall grass can support a bird or two in winter.

East of the Cascades the species is less common but it can still be found locally in marshes and in grassy areas along rivers and lakes. Most birds are at lower elevations, and colder areas often have no wrens even if the habitat looks otherwise appropriate. The species is easiest to find along the Columbia-Snake system and at major marshes, lakes, and reservoirs, where it is uncommon to locally abundant.

The species is increasing in winter throughout the region according to CBC trend data. This may reflect better observer coverage of the habitats that the species prefers or it may be a genuine population increase.

Location	Trend	Circles	Birds/100 ph
BC	2.6	18	0.42
WA	1.6	30	0.88
OR	7.2	36	1.61
ALL	2.0	790	0.86

Family Cinclidae

American Dipper
Cinclus mexicanus

This species stays in and next to fast-moving streams, and some birds remain at high elevations in winter. Others come downslope, appearing along fast rivers and creeks that remain open in winter. Because so many birds remain at higher elevations where CBCs are few, count data is of limited value in considering the species' abundance or relative density.

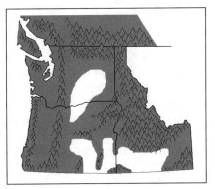

Some birds are found to sea level where small creeks empty directly into the ocean, and birds sometimes concentrate where salmon are spawning.

Location	Trend	Circles	Birds/100 ph
BC	-1.8	40	1.14
WA	1.4	19	0.42
OR	1.0	33	1.00
ALL	0.7	285	0.79

Family Regulidae

Golden-crowned Kinglet
Regulus satrapa

This species can be found in winter in most of the region wherever there are coniferous trees, although there are few birds at high elevations. Some birds come into lowland deciduous woodlands with flocks of other small birds such as chickadees,

nuthatches, and Ruby-crowned Kinglets.

Location	Trend	Circles	Birds/100 ph
OR	1.4	42	13.87
WA	6.5	34	14.77
BC	3.4	46	14.79
ID	1.7	14	2.71
ALL	2.5	1827	2.86

At middle elevations in the coast ranges and mountain foothills below the snow line, these birds can be abundant, as they also can in the western interior valleys and on the coast where appropriate habitat exists. Flocks of several dozen birds are common, especially mixed with other small forest birds.

Away from forested areas this species is much less common, with small numbers of birds appearing at isolated groves (including juniper) occasionally. They are occasional in eastern Idaho and uncommon in western Idaho.

CBC trend data shows a regionwide increase in wintering birds.

Golden-crowned Kinglets

Ruby-crowned Kinglet
Regulus calendula

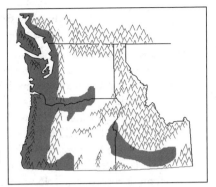

This species is abundant west of the high Cascades in winter, and widespread but uncommon at low elevations east of the mountains. This is one of the most abundant birds in the western lowlands and coast ranges in winter, forming small flocks and also feeding with Golden-crowned Kinglets, chickadees, and nuthatches. A number of these birds also forage alone in winter, and they can be found in almost any clump of bushes or grove of trees from the Cascade foothills west to the coast.

East of the Cascades these birds remain mainly in low-elevation riparian areas and in towns and cities. They are often absent in winter, especially away from these areas of warmer temperatures and available food. The species is occasional to rare and often absent from northeastern Washington, northern Idaho, northeastern Oregon, and southern British Columbia in winter.

Populations that breed in the Northwest winter to the south, and birds that winter in the region are thought to come primarily from southern Alaska and British Columbia based on specimen evidence.

Except for a slight decrease in British Columbia, CBC trend data shows a regionwide increase.

Location	Trend	Circles	Birds/100 ph
BC	-0.4	30	1.30
ID	1.3	14	0.56
WA	3.0	33	4.34
OR	3.6	41	5.37
ALL	1.6	1520	3.56

Family Sylviidae

Blue-gray Gnatcatcher
Polioptila caerulea

This species is rare in winter, mainly in western Oregon, where there are a few records. It is noteworthy that most extralimital reports of this species in the region have come in late fall and winter, perhaps as a consequence of some post-breeding adults moving in the wrong direction or of some young birds dispersing northward by mistake.

One was in Vancouver, BC, from November 19 to December 1, 1981. There are three records for Washington, including a late November record. The two winter records were February 21, 1993, at Bottle Beach, Ocosta, Grays Harbor County, and at the University of Washington arboretum from December 6, 1986, through January 30, 1987 (Tweit and Skriletz 1996).

Family Turdidae

Western Bluebird
Sialia mexicana

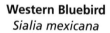

The Western Bluebird is common to occasional and local west of the high Cascades in Oregon, uncommon to occasional and local east of the Cascades throughout the region. This species is most common in the oak-dominated hillsides of southwestern Oregon, with smaller populations extending up both sides of the Willamette Valley to the hills south of Portland.

Within the southwestern corner of Oregon the species can be locally abundant, but farther north it becomes more local. North of the northern Willamette Valley it becomes quite rare, and it is rare in western Washington (absent in some areas) and British Columbia.

Location	Trend	Circles	Birds/100 ph
OR	1.3	32	1.51
ALL	1.2	277	4.87

East of the Cascades this breeder departs in winter, with a few birds remaining in mild years, mainly in junipers with other frugivores. A few remain regularly in the Okanagan Valley. Most winter records of large numbers are from the vicinity of Bend, OR, where large juniper stands attract many bluebirds, solitaires and robins.

Mountain Bluebird
Sialia currucoides

This bluebird is uncommon to occasional except in mild years, mainly in central Oregon. It is rare in the Okanagan Valley, eastern Washington, and southern Idaho and occasional in southern Oregon east of the Cascades.

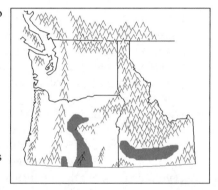

This breeder usually leaves in winter, but a few birds remain, especially in mild years. Those that stay tend to frequent juniper groves and other trees bearing fruit or berries, sometimes with groups of robins or solitaires. In some years hundreds of birds can be found in central Oregon in the vicinity of Bend, but in other years the species is absent. Northbound migrants often pass through southeastern Oregon and southern Idaho by late February, and some may reach British Columbia before the end of the month.

It is rare in winter west of the Cascades, mainly in southwestern Oregon.

Location	Trend	Circles	Birds/100 ph
OR	-0.8	18	4.55
ALL	0.4	318	3.95

Townsend's Solitaire
Myadestes townsendi

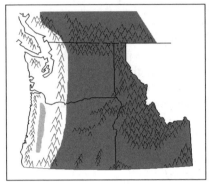

This species is locally abundant in juniper groves east of the Cascades, and can be found in small numbers in the coast ranges in winter. Hundreds of solitaires move out of the mountains in winter and form loose flocks, sometimes with robins, in juniper groves throughout the region east of the Cascades. Some move into towns and feed on ornamental plantings.

West of the high Cascades a few birds can be found in winter, mainly in clear-cuts. A small population breeds in the coast ranges and a few birds can be found there in winter as well, sometimes occurring to the coast. CBC data suggest that the species is more regular on the coast in Oregon than in Washington, perhaps because there are more Oregon coast CBCs located adjacent to high-elevation areas where the species breeds, while counts on the southern Washington coast include mainly low foothills inland. The species does breed in the Olympic range, but the winter status of these birds is not well known.

There are a few birds reported each year in the western interior valleys and along Puget Sound. One or two birds were nearly annual on Bellingham, WA, CBCs in the 1970s and early 1980s, but the species has been absent in most years since.

Location	Trend	Circles	Birds/100 ph
BC	-0.6	25	0.62
ID	1.6	14	0.91
WA	0.0	21	0.38
OR	2.5	33	8.58
ALL	1.5	479	1.64

Swainson's Thrush
Catharus ustulatus

Although there are numerous CBC reports of the species in the region, no confirmed record exists in the region in winter. A bird was collected at Arcata on the northern California coast on January 23, 1990 (Harris 1996), so a future confirmed report from the Northwest is possible.

Hermit Thrush
Catharus guttatus

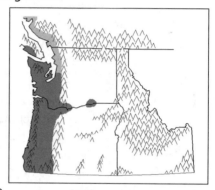

This species is locally common on the southern Oregon coast, uncommon elsewhere in the region west of the Cascades, and occasional east of the Cascades. The birds that winter along the coast and in the western interior valleys are mostly from populations that breed in Alaska and British Columbia, according to specimen data (Gabrielson and Jewett 1940, Jewett et al. 1953, AOU 1957). There are a few records of the subspecies that breed in the region also wintering here. The small number that can sometimes be found east of the Cascades in winter are not of well-known origin.

CBC numbers on the southern Oregon coast can approach and even exceed one hundred birds in peak years, but a few dozen is a more common count. The species is progressively less abundant farther north, and is uncommon to occasional in western British Columbia and northwestern Washington in winter.

Location	Trend	Circles	Birds/100 ph
BC	-0.2	18	0.73
WA	2.2	28	0.17
OR	2.1	31	0.70
ALL	1.3	1274	0.79

Most CBCs east of the Cascades do not report the species, but it is uncommon and found regularly along the Columbia River east to the Tri-Cities, WA, area, and is present in some years in the Klamath Basin, at Bend, OR, and locally elsewhere, mainly in riparian areas and cities. It is a rare lingerer to inland British Columbia and rare in Idaho in winter.

The table below shows the relative increase in numbers southward using data from four counts of long standing.

Count	Average tally
Campbell River, BC	0.2
Bellingham, WA	0.6
Grays Harbor, WA	5.5
Coos Bay, OR	22.2

Dusky Thrush
Turdus naumanni

This is a rare winter vagrant; there is one record from British Columbia. A single bird was at Langley from January 2 to April 19, 1993.

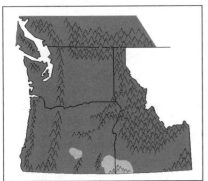

American Robin
Turdus migratorius

The robin is one of the most widespread and, in some areas, abundant wintering birds in the region. Most winter birds come from breeding grounds north of the region, and the species can be found by the hundreds, sometimes thousands, at favored areas west of the Cascades and in juniper groves east of the mountains.

East of the Cascades the species is sometimes found with Townsend's Solitaires in winter. Almost every area in the region, even the coldest, has at least a few wintering robins living, it seems, in trees such as mountain ash and juniper. At Bend, OR, thousands of birds sometimes gather in juniper groves.

Location	Trend	Circles	Birds/100 ph
BC	-3.7	42	25.19
ID	5.2	16	17.51
WA	1.0	36	54.04
OR	-3.6	45	132.74
ALL	0.8	1998	172.71

West of the Cascades robins gather by the hundreds throughout the western interior valleys and lowlands to the coast. In some areas they can be found spread out over wet pastures, feeding with Killdeer, starlings, and other species. Robins winter in large numbers in towns and cities, where they eat berries, fruit, worms, and other soft foods. Most birds remain at lower elevations and do not winter in the high mountains.

Varied Thrush
Ixoreus naevius

This species is common in winter west of the high Cascades and locally in eastern Washington, BC, northeastern Oregon, and northern Idaho. In some years hundreds of birds can be found on CBCs along the coast and in the western interior valleys, but in other years only a few are present. This variation also occurs east

of the Cascades and may be explainable by variations in the severity of winter weather or snow levels, or the local availability of food.

Location	Trend	Circles	Birds/100 ph
BC	-3.0	44	3.33
WA	1.3	35	3.61
OR	-1.7	37	7.39
ALL	-0.5	384	1.05

Varied Thrush

The species is usually much less common east of the Cascades than on the west side, but it is nonetheless usually present at some locales with plenty of dense cover. It is common to uncommon along the northeastern Columbia-Snake system and in nearby areas of eastern Washington and in lowland areas of northern and (locally) southwestern Idaho. It is uncommon to occasional along the lower east side of the Cascades north into the Okanagan at CBCs such as Penticton, BC, Vernon, BC, Ellensburg, WA, Bend, OR, and Klamath Falls, OR.

Varied Thrushes can be found in some years in very small numbers in other relatively low-lying valleys such as the Yakima and John Day valleys. They are usually absent from the higher valleys of northeastern Oregon (they have been recorded five times on the Baker, OR, CBC between 1957 and 1991, and are very rare at LaGrande) and are rare south to Malheur NWR and Summer Lake.

Subfamily Timaliidae

Wrentit
Chamaea fasciata

Wrentits are common in dense thickets along the Oregon coast and in the southwestern interior valleys, foothills, and coast ranges. The statement in Root (1988) that "[i]ts distribution runs from the Strait of Juan de Fuca between Washington and Vancouver Island down the entire length of the coast to Mexico" is not correct. In fact, the species does not occur in Washington at all, let alone to the strait. Wrentits have perhaps the most abrupt range

Location	Trend	Circles	Birds/100 ph
OR	1.4	18	3.40
ALL	1.7	122	2.77

termination of any bird found in the region—they literally stop at the Columbia River.

Although the species is most common on the southern and central coast, it is relatively easy to find north to the Columbia. The inland population is common in the Rogue and Umpqua valleys and north to southern Lane County. Birds of indeterminate subspecies are found from Lane County north locally to central Polk and southeastern Linn County, and the species is apparently continuing to expand northward. It is occasional locally in southwestern Klamath County in the Klamath River canyon. The prevailing theory of its expansion is that it moves mainly through overgrown clear-cuts and burns.

Family Mimidae

Gray Catbird
Dumetella carolinensis

This is a rare lingerer in winter. It has been recorded at Coeur d'Alene, ID, on December 18, 1993, and one that "ate berries in LaGrande," Union County, OR, wintered in 1988-89 (Gilligan et al. 1994). A bird wintered in Corvallis, OR, in 1997. There are three winter records from the interior valleys of British Columbia.

Northern Mockingbird
Mimus polyglottos

This species is uncommon to occasional in the Rogue Valley in winter, where it has become somewhat more common in recent years. It is occasional elsewhere in southwestern Oregon and occasional to rare elsewhere in the region in winter.

A small but significant northward dispersal of mockingbirds occurs in fall and winter into the region, with birds sometimes reaching Idaho and Washington. It is very rare to British Columbia.

Sage Thrasher
Oreoscoptes montanus

This semi-hardy species winters mainly south of the region, but a few birds can sometimes be found in southeastern Oregon, especially in mild years. This species is a relatively early northbound migrant, and a few outriders can begin appearing in February, although most do not come until late March. It is absent from Idaho, Washington, and British Columbia in winter.

Brown Thrasher
Toxostoma rufum

This eastern species is rare at any season in the region, but there are a number of records from winter. There are about seven winter records in Oregon.

One was at found at a feeder in Reardan, Spokane County, WA, from January 1 through February 19, 1996. One was near Fort Hall in southeastern Idaho on January 14, 1987. One was in West Vancouver, BC, on February 23, 1972.

Brown Thrasher

Spokane, WA, February 4, 1996 (Photograph by Patrick Sullivan)

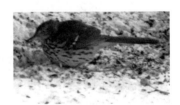

Family Sturnidae

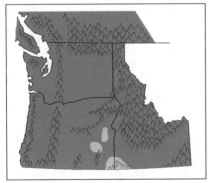

European Starling
Sturnus vulgaris

This abundant widespread introduced species occurs throughout the region in winter except in heavily forested or completely open areas. It forms large flocks in winter, and many birds move to the valleys and cities where they infest feedlots, agricultural areas, parks, and Russian-olive groves east of the Cascades.

Location	Trend	Circles	Birds/100 ph
BC	-3.8	47	190.90
ID	-4.1	18	299.04
WA	3.3	35	336.38
OR	-2.0	45	405.36
ALL	2.0	2110	1345.86

Although the abundance of this species varies somewhat from year to year, it is usually either abundant or extremely abundant. In some areas starlings are the most common winter bird where large roosts form. However, the Northwest (except for Washington) has seen a decrease in Starling numbers on CBCs in the past thirty years, a small piece of good news.

Although some birds remain at higher elevations and away from concentration areas, most gather in large flocks.

Crested Myna
Acridotheres cristatellus

This is an introduced resident in Vancouver and northern Richmond, BC.

Family Prunellidae

Siberian Accentor
Prunella montanella

This is a rare winter vagrant. There is one record from British Columbia: a single bird at Everett Crowley Park, Vancouver, on December 15, 1993. Another wintered near Ketchum, ID, in 1997.

Siberian Accentor

Ketchum, ID, 1997
(Photograph by Laurie Barrera)

Family Motacillidae

White Wagtail
Motacilla alba

The region's only winter record of a bird reliably identified as this species is of one first found at Crockett Lake, Whidbey Island, WA, on January 14, 1984. Although the bird was in immature plumage when found, it remained through May and was identifiable after molting into adult plumage, when it proved to be a male of this species (Tweit and Skriletz 1996)

Black-backed Wagtail
Motacilla lugens

A bird at Eugene, OR, from February 3 to March 26, 1974, is the only certain winter record from the region, but a wagtail that was either this species or a White Wagtail (*M. alba*) was at Umatilla NWR, OR, on February 9, 1975.

Red-throated Pipit
Anthus cervinus

This bird is a vagrant. One was at Boundary Bay, BC, from December 22 to 28, 1990.

American Pipit
Anthus rubescens

This species can be locally abundant, especially west of the Cascades, where it winters in large flocks on recently tilled fields, ryegrass fields, mudflats, and other open locations with little or no vegetation.

East of the Cascades it occurs in similar settings, but usually in lesser numbers and more locally. It is usually absent from higher elevations, occurring mainly in river valleys and lake basins. The species can be found in winter locally throughout the region except in mountainous areas, but it is absent from most of northern and central Idaho.

Location	Trend	Circles	Birds/100 ph
BC	-0.6	15	1.08
WA	3.0	17	0.59
OR	1.3	33	1.18
ALL	-2.1	938	7.33

Family Bombycillidae

Bohemian Waxwing
Bombycilla garrulus

This irruptive species is abundant to common in most years in southern interior British Columbia, northeastern Washington, most of Idaho, and northeastern Oregon. Although determining abundance of irruptive species is always difficult, the region in general shows the same slight decline noted across the continent.

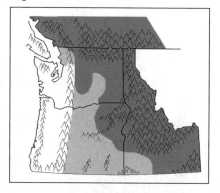

In most years flocks of scores to hundreds of birds descend on the northeastern part of the region, feeding most obviously in ornamental plantings such as mountain ash trees, holly, and other fruit-bearing trees.

During invasion years these birds extend their incursions farther into the region, reaching most of Oregon and Washington east of the Cascades, locally in the hundreds. Numbers vary considerably by year and location. During these peak years a few birds reach western Oregon and Washington, but in most years the species is rare west of the Cascades throughout the region. During the winter of 1968-69 hundreds

Location	Trend	Circles	Birds/100 ph
BC	-0.8	34	54.46
ID	0.3	16	62.89
WA	-3.4	19	75.24
OR	-4.3	22	9.14
ALL	-1.0	599	24.37

Frequency of occurrence on sample CBCs	
Penticton, BC	100%
Vaseux Lake, BC	95%
Ellensburg, WA	82%
Tri-Cities, WA	55%
Union County, OR	78%
John Day, OR	50%
Boise, ID	70%
Pocatello, ID	77%

of birds occurred to the western interior valleys, but no western invasion of this magnitude has since been recorded. The table shows the pattern of occurrence at sites within the species' regular winter range.

CBC trend data indicate that while Idaho numbers have been increasing slightly, numbers elsewhere in the region have not. This may simply be a matter of birds stopping farther east in their irruptions.

Cedar Waxwing
Bombycilla cedrorum

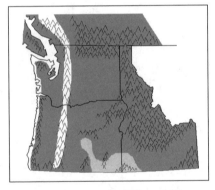

This species is locally common to abundant throughout the region, but is sometimes absent from certain areas, especially the coast. It is not found in dense forests even at low elevations, and is most common in areas with abundant natural or introduced berry-producing trees and shrubs such as mountain ash and juniper. It can also be found using fruit trees, where it sometimes feeds with robins and other birds.

Numbers vary considerably from year to year as the birds follow the availability of food. As a consequence, large flocks can be found in one place while nearby locations have none at all. In most years it is rare east of the Cascades in British

Location	Trend	Circles	Birds/100 ph
BC	-4.4	29	2.13
WA	-2.0	31	13.22
OR	1.9	41	7.92
ALL	2.7	1778	11.54

Columbia, montane Idaho, and northern and central Washington, becoming more common farther south. However, the availability of abundant berries is more important than temperature or latitude, and large numbers sometimes winter at northerly locations when food crops permit: hundreds can be found in Spokane, WA, in most winters because the city has many fruit-bearing trees.

Cedar Waxwings

Family Ptilogonatidae

Phainopepla
Phainopepla nitens

Phainopepla

*Jackson
County, OR,
December
1988
(Photograph
by Bill Stotz)*

This vagrant has been found once in winter in the Rogue Valley, where a young male remained from December 22, 1988, to January 1, 1989, 14 miles east of Gold Hill, Jackson County. In addition, one was at Stanley Park, Vancouver, BC, on January 17 and 20, 1993.

Family Parulidae

Tennessee Warbler
Vermivora peregrina

This bird is a rare vagrant in the region in winter, mainly in southwestern Oregon. Birds have been found on the Florence, OR, CBC in 1987 and 1988. A bird was found at Florence on December 29, 1980, and one was at Eugene, Lane County, November 29+ 1981. A single bird was found at the same site in Newport, Lincoln County, OR, on January 4-14, 1992, and again February 11, 1993. One was near Satsop, Grays Harbor County, WA, from December 5, 1993, through January 5, 1994 (Tweit and Skriletz 1996).

Orange-crowned Warbler
Vermivora celata

This uncommon semi-hardy warbler can be found in small numbers in western Oregon and Washington every year, and in western British Columbia occasionally. It is most regular on the coast and in southwestern Oregon, and is less often reported north of Seattle.

Knowledge of the winter distribution of this species is colored by the fact that it prefers a habitat type that is usually undercovered by observers, even on CBCs. It is found most often in dense lowland brush such as willow and blackberry tangles that require careful attention to cover thoroughly. It also uses plantings in urban areas. (See Irons and Fix (1990) for a good description of the habitat preferred by this and other less common winterers.) Because of this preference it tends to be found most regularly on CBCs that can field a large numbers of observers (e.g., Eugene OR, averaging 1.8 birds per count with a high of eight) than on counts with plenty of good habitat but fewer observers (e.g. Coos Bay, OR, which misses the species on most counts but where it is surely present in small numbers each year).

In mild years this species can be found east of the Cascades, especially in the Columbia River lowlands east to the Tri-Cities, WA, area. There are a few early-winter records for the Snake River valley east to southern Idaho. It is usually absent from northern Washington and inland British Columbia in winter, but there is one record for the Okanagan Valley, BC.

Location	Trend	Circles	Birds/100 ph
WA	0.2	14	0.04
OR	0.1	17	0.04
ALL	-0.3	596	0.78

Nashville Warbler
Vermivora ruficapilla

This species is rare in the region in winter, with a few Oregon records from west of the Cascades, mainly on the coast. There is one early-winter record from the Boise, ID, area. One was in Victoria, BC, from December 19, 1989, to January 31, 1990.

Lucy's Warbler
Vermivora luciae

This bird is a rare winter vagrant. One record for the region, a bird photographed along the north fork of the Siuslaw River, Lane County, OR, from December 27, 1986, to January 24, 1987, has been accepted by the OBRC. See Bond (1987) for details.

Northern Parula
Parula americana

This is a rare winter vagrant. One wintered at Richland, Benton County, WA, from January 10 to February 3, 1975. This was accepted by the WBRC as the state's first record.

Yellow Warbler
Dendroica petechia

Although there have been many CBC reports from the region, mainly from sites west of the Cascades, very few are documented. Gilligan et al. (1994) note that "there are several verified records to at least late December in the Willamette Valley." There are a few generally accepted records on the southern Oregon coast. The similarity of some races of Orange-crowned Warbler makes many reports of this species suspect.

Cape May Warbler
Dendroica tigrina

A rare winter vagrant. There is one winter record for the region. One was at Dover, ID (the state's first documented record) in January 1980, although the photograph taken at a feeder was not discovered and published until 1995 (*NAS Field Notes* 49(5): 953).

Black-throated Blue Warbler
Dendroica caerulescens

A rare winter vagrant. There are a few well-documented winter records for the region. One was collected near Lewiston, ID, on January 10, 1955 (Taylor and Trost 1987). A male was on Mercer Island, King County, WA, from November 2, 1994, until at least April 5, 1995 (Tweit and Skriletz 1996, Phil Mattocks, personal communication). There are three winter records of males for Oregon, as follows. One was at Medford, Jackson County, from January 9 to 30, 1986. Another was at Powers, Coos County, January 20-29, 1989. The third was at Bayocean Peninsula, Tillamook County, on December 11, 1985.

In British Columbia, there is one record of an adult male wintering at Nakusp from December 12, 1993, to January 16, 1994, when it killed itself flying into a window (specimen #15172 at Cowan Vertebrate Museum).

Yellow-rumped Warbler
Dendroica coronata

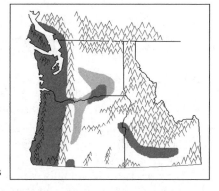

This is the only relatively common widespread warbler in winter in the region. It ranges in density from rare or absent in most of the high-elevation areas east of the Cascades to locally abundant on the outer coast.

The species is rare to occasional in interior British Columbia (five winter records in the Okanagan noted by Cannings et al. (1987), but many more since), northeastern Washington (four records in thirty years on the Spokane CBC), and most of northern Idaho. It can, however, be uncommon to locally common not too far away in the Columbia-Snake bottomlands, where scores, sometimes hundreds, of birds are sometimes found on the Tri-Cities, WA, CBC and at other locales.

This Columbia River wintering area is the only significant winter range east of the Cascades. Farther south in eastern Oregon and southern Idaho the species is occasional to rare,

	Avg	High	Low
Campbell River, BC	.2	1	0
Bellingham, WA	7.3	33	0
Seattle, WA	8.6	34	0
Grays Harbor, WA	500	1248	0
Portland, OR	40.1	209	0
Tillamook Bay, OR	22.6	119	0
Coos Bay, OR	693	1742	7

mainly in warmer lowland areas. In mild years it can be found fairly easily in the Snake River valley. Even in the Klamath Basin the species is quite hard to find in winter.

West of the Cascades numbers vary considerably from year to year. At Puget Sound CBCs the species can be absent, but usually a few birds and sometimes several dozen can be found. Farther south at inland locations the species is more common, especially in southwestern Oregon.

On the outer coast these warblers can be locally abundant or nearly absent from year to year. The table shows some of the ranges both inland and along the coast.

A few northbound migrants begin appearing in the southern part of the region by late February.

Black-throated Gray Warbler
Dendroica nigrescens

This warbler is rare in winter, with a few records west of the Cascades. There are eight Oregon CBC records of single birds; five in the western interior valleys and three on coastal counts. There are three Washington CBC records, two in Seattle and one at Grays Harbor. Gilligan et al. (1994) note that there have been about fifteen winter records in western Oregon since 1972.

There is one British Columbia record from Swan Lake, Saanich, on December 18, 1994.

Townsend's Warbler
Dendroica townsendi

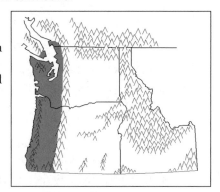

The Townsend's Warbler is locally common west of the Cascades in winter, mainly on the Oregon coast. A few of these birds can often be found in flocks of chickadees and kinglets in winter, and sometimes large pure flocks of fifty or more Townsend's Warblers are found, moving through the trees like kinglets.These flocks sometimes contain rare overwintering birds such as Hermit or Black-throated Gray Warblers.

East of the Cascades this species is very rare in winter, probably as a late migrant. One was at Pendleton, Umatilla County, OR, on December 12, 1953 (Burleigh 1957), a northeasterly site for so late in the season.

Townsend's Warbler

211

Location	Trend	Circles	Birds/100 ph
OR	3.9	21	0.35
WA	1.9	16	0.28
ALL	5.5	163	0.26

In British Columbia, the species is a rare winterer on the southwest coast and southern Vancouver Island; it is absent from the interior.

Hermit Warbler
Dendroica occidentalis

This warbler is rare in winter in western Oregon, where there are several records, most on CBCs, on which there are ten records. Unlike some semi-hardy species, this warbler (like the Black-throated Gray) has been found more often in the western interior valleys on Oregon CBCs (six records) than on coastal counts (four records). It is not found every year in the region. When it does occur, it is usually found with flocks of Townsend's Warblers and other forest feeders.

Blackburnian Warbler
Dendroica fusca

This is a vagrant. One male spent the winter of 1987-88 in a farmyard east of Nehalem, Tillamook County, OR, from November 15, 1987, to March 12+ 1988. Photos of the bird have been accepted by the OBRC.

Blackburnian Warbler

Nehalem, OR, winter 1987-88
(Photograph by Harry B. Nehls)

Yellow-throated Warbler
Dendroica dominica

A vagrant. There is one winter record from Idaho near Harrison on December 31, 1995.

Yellow-throated Warbler

Harrison, ID, December 31, 1995
(Photograph by George Oatman)

Prairie Warbler
Dendroica discolor

A rare winter vagrant. One was at Wallula, Walla Walla County, WA, on December 20, 1989. A male was at South Beach, Lincoln County, OR, from December 10+ 1995.

There is one noteworthy extralimital record from Queen Charlotte Islands, northern British Columbia at Masset, from December 18, 1993, to January 25, 1994.

Prairie Warbler

South Beach, OR,
December 1995
(Photograph by Eric Horvath)

Palm Warbler
Dendroica palmarum

This species was considered rare in the region until the early 1970s, when it began being reported annually along the outer coast, especially in Washington. It is now occasional, found regularly from early fall through winter along the region's coast, and rarely inland. It is generally more common along the Oregon

and southern Washington coast and is less often reported in British Columbia. Single birds are now found in most years on three or four coastal CBCs, and in peak years multiple birds have been found at some counts. The peak count for the region in winter is the six at Coquille Valley, OR, in 1993. Grays Harbor, WA, had five in 1976.

It is very rare east of the Cascades in winter, with a record at the mouth of the Deschutes River, Sherman County, OR, on February 2, 1992.

Black-and-White Warbler

Seattle, WA, December 6, 1996
(Photograph by Ruth Sullivan)

Black-and-white Warbler
Mniotilta varia

A vagrant. One was observed from December 17, 1977, to January 22+, 1978, in Coos Bay, OR; photos were accepted by the OBRC. Another was at Eugene, OR, from February 25, 1989, through the end of winter (Gilligan et al. 1994). A recent Seattle record appears in the photo.

There are two winter records for British Columbia: one was at Vancouver from December 15, 1991, to February 1992.

American Redstart
Setophaga ruticilla

Two birds were reported at Coos Bay, OR, on January 13, 1980, and one was at Eugene, OR, on December 28, 1987 (Gilligan et al. 1994).

Northern Waterthrush
Seiurus noveboracensis

This species is extremely rare in winter. The most recent record was at the Skagit Wildlife Management Area, WA, on December 14, 1996 (*Washington Ornithological Society News* No. 47). There are three previous Washington records: December 15, 1968, in Seattle, January 24, 1974, at the Skagit Game Range, and December 30, 1978, in King County.

One was on the Tillamook, OR, CBC in December 1995. Another was a window-kill in Coos Bay, OR, on January 7, 1978. One was reported on the Malheur NWR, OR, CBC in 1963, but details are unavailable.

Northern Waterthrush

Skagit WMA, WA
December 14, 1996
(Photograph by Ruth
Sullivan)

One was "seen in a spring-fed thicket at Oliver on the Oliver-Osoyoos CBC" in British Columbia on December 28, 1983, and was also present the following day (Cannings et al., 1987). The species has been reported once on the American Falls, ID, CBC.

MacGillivray's Warbler
Oporornis tolmiei

Two birds were found on the Eugene, OR, CBC in 1967, one of which was sheltering in a garage. There have been other reports in winter. The species is very rare in winter and all records should be documented.

Common Yellowthroat
Geothlypis trichas

This species is rare in winter, but a few birds remain in most years, mainly at lowland sites west of the Cascades. There are several CBC records for Oregon and Washington. The only published record for Oregon east of the Cascades of which I am aware is of a bird at John Day, Grant County, on December 8, 1987. In British Columbia, the species is a rare winterer in the southwest (five to six records) and a winter vagrant to the Okanagan Valley (two records).

Hooded Warbler
Wilsonia citrina

This bird is a rare winter vagrant found to date only in Washington. One was at Seattle, King County, from December 31, 1975, to April 4, 1976 (accepted by the WBRC as the first state record). A male was at Pullman, WA, from November 30 to December 11, 1989.

Wilson's Warbler
Wilsonia pusilla

Although this species is reported occasionally on CBCs, very few records have been adequately documented. One bird was collected on December 6, 1955, near Coquille, Coos County, OR (Burleigh 1957). The only winter record east of the Cascades in Oregon was a bird at Weston, Umatilla County, on January 14, 1990 (Gilligan et al. 1994). A male was found December 9, 1964, at Kelowna in the Okanagan Valley, BC, and there are two winter records from Vancouver and one from Vernon, BC.

Yellow-breasted Chat
Icteria virens

There are only three winter records known to me, all in southwestern Oregon. One was seen January 11, 1956, eating pears in the Rogue Valley (Gilligan et al. 1994) and another was noted by several observers at Bandon, Coos County, on December 29, 1991. The most recent record was of a bird that remained at Ashland, Jackson County, from December 14, 1994, to January 25, 1995 (*Audubon Field Notes* 49(2): 191).

Family Thraupidae

Western Tanager
Piranga ludoviciana

This bird is very rare in winter, with a few generally accepted records west of the Cascades. There are two winter records from southwestern British Columbia and two Washington CBC records in the data period. Very few generally accepted winter records exist for Oregon. The four reported on the 1941 Portland CBC are probably erroneous.

Family Emberizidae

Green-tailed Towhee
Pipilo chlorurus

This towhee is extremely rare in winter. There is one winter record for Oregon, a bird that frequented a feeder at the town of Riverside near Coquille, Coos County, in December 1994. One was on the Pocatello, ID, CBC in 1974.

Spotted Towhee
Pipilo maculatus

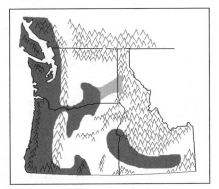

This species is abundant from the western interior valleys to the coast, with several birds to be found in almost any blackberry patch or in other dense shrubbery. CBC tallies in the hundreds in lowland areas are common. West of the Cascades the species is almost uniformly abundant from southwestern British Columbia to the California line. No major local centers of abundance appear except where CBCs fielding many observers in prime habitat naturally find plenty of birds. A few remain in the western Cascades.

East of the Cascades most towhees leave in winter, but some remain, mainly in lowland riparian areas and towns. The species is absent on most CBCs in northern Idaho and eastern Washington, and is rare in transmontane British Columbia. Counts such as Spokane, WA (2.2 birds per year, often absent) and Tri-Cities, WA (1.7 birds per year, often absent) show that towhees do not follow the pattern of some species such as Yellow-rumped Warbler that remain in numbers at northerly locales along the Columbia bottoms.

In eastern Oregon and southern Idaho the pattern is the same, with even southerly sites such as Adel, OR, rarely reporting the species. At Pocatello, ID, towhees have been found on 59 percent of CBCs in the twenty-nine-year history of the count. Only along the eastern base of the Cascades (Bend, Klamath Falls) do eastside CBCs find the species annually, sometimes in the double digits.

Location	Trend	Circles	Birds/100 ph
BC	0.2	30	4.67
WA	1.1	34	4.18
OR	1.8	38	3.86
ALL	-1.1	1583	2.76

California Towhee
Pipilo crissalis

This bird is a common resident of the Rogue Valley and adjacent areas in southwestern Oregon, where it can be found in almost any dense underbrush, especially in ceanothus. Medford averages 22.9 birds on the CBC and Grants Pass averages 9.6 birds, probably reflecting both variations in available habitat and observer coverage.

It is local and uncommon east to southwestern Klamath County, OR, and local and occasional north to southern Douglas County, OR. The Klamath Falls CBC finds one occasionally, but most birds are farther southwest in the Klamath River canyon and vicinity. They can also be found locally just south of the border at Lava Beds National Monument, CA.

American Tree Sparrow
Spizella arborea

This sparrow occurs in the region only in winter, with most birds in eastern Washington, Idaho, and northeastern Oregon. Numbers vary considerably from year to year and long-term trends can be seen in some areas. Cannings et al. (1987) offer the following comment about winter numbers in the Okanagan Valley:

> An interesting point that emerges from analysis of earlier Penticton-Summerland CBCs is that tree sparrows were perhaps more common in the first half of the twentieth century than they are today. From 1926 to 1949, despite much less observer coverage, they were seen almost twice as often and in more than three times the numbers of recent decades.

Count	% with Tree Sparrows
Penticton, BC	38
Tri-Cities, WA	10
Moscow, ID	38
American Falls, ID	94
Baker Valley, OR	60
Malheur NWR, OR	37

At other sites the species has become more common from the 1960s through the 1980s, e.g., Malheur NWR, OR, where it was found only twice in twenty years through the 1970s, but was been found eight out of ten years in the 1980s, twice in double digits.

This species is more regular and more common farther east in the region. It is found much more often in Idaho than in central Oregon at a similar latitude, and is often present by the score in eastern Idaho and northeastern Oregon.

West of the Cascades the species is annual in winter in southwestern British Columbia and extreme northern Washington. It is nearly annual on the Bellingham, WA, CBC but much less common farther south. It is rare in winter in southwestern Washington and western Oregon. There are very few records for the coast of Oregon or Washington.

Location	Trend	Circles	Birds/100 ph
BC	0.4	25	0.62
ID	1.2	16	9.61
WA	-2.8	15	0.46
OR	1.0	16	1.76
ALL	-2.1	1473	25.89

Chipping Sparrow
Spizella passerina

This sparrow is rare in winter, with most records from southwestern Oregon. The species is a rare lingerer in the southern interior valleys of British Columbia in the winter with at least three records. It is reported on CBCs far more often than it actually occurs, but there are many legitimate winter records in the region.

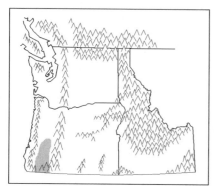

The status of the species is clouded by the possibility that some reports refer to misidentified Clay-colored Sparrows, which are almost as likely in winter west of the Cascades. It is also likely that less experienced observers familiar with Chipping Sparrows in summer sometimes misidentify American Tree Sparrows or immature White-crowned Sparrows as Chipping Sparrows.

Clay-colored Sparrow
Spizella pallida

This species is rare but almost annual in western Oregon in winter. There are at least ten winter records in western Oregon since 1980. The species is very rare in Washington. There are no winter records yet for eastern Oregon or Idaho. In British Columbia, the species has been found three times in the Delta / Ladner area south of Vancouver in winter.

Vesper Sparrow
Pooecetes gramineus

This species departs from the region in winter, but in mild years a few sometimes remain, mainly in Oregon. There is one winter record from the Victoria area, Vancouver Island, BC. Even in the colder parts of the region there are occasional winter reports, though some of these may be referable to misidentified longspurs, Horned Larks, or other species.

Lark Sparrow
Chondestes grammacus

This species is common in the eastern Rogue Valley, OR, in winter, but only occasional in the Grants Pass, OR, area. The Medford, OR, CBC averages 33 birds per CBC with a high of 142.

Birds are occasionally found north to southern Douglas County, OR, in winter, and wanderers appear here and there, mainly in southwestern Oregon.

Sage Sparrow
Amphispiza belli

Most of these desert sparrows leave the region in winter, but a few remain in mild years, mainly in south-central Oregon. Because of limited field activity in the Great Basin in winter, reports tend to come from Oregon CBCs such as Hart Mountain, Summer Lake and the two Malheur NWR counts. Birds begin returning from the south by late February.

Lark Bunting
Calamospiza melanocorys

This is a rare winter vagrant. One female was found near Oakville, Linn County, OR, on January 2, 1967, during the Corvallis CBC. It was subsequently collected, and the specimen is now in the Fish and Wildlife Museum at Oregon State University (FWNO 7597) (*Oregon Birds* 20(3):84).

Savannah Sparrow
Passerculus sandwichensis

Most of these sparrows leave the region in winter, but the Rogue Valley of southwestern Oregon is a significant wintering ground where scores can often be found. Smaller numbers can usually be found in the western interior valleys and along the coast north to southwestern British Columbia. They can be

locally common in lowland areas with plenty of good habitat, such as at Ridgefield NWR, WA, and Sauvie Island, OR, along the Columbia River. In 1996-97 a flock of over two hundred birds could be found regularly in Linn County, OR. At coastal sites they are often located in dense beach grass as well as in the moist overgrown pastures and similar sites that they prefer.

East of the Cascades they are much less regular, with an occasional bird appearing, mainly in lake basins and riverbottom areas. Only along the Columbia River to southeastern Washington and in the Klamath Basin is the species fairly regular in winter. Otherwise it is rare in winter east of the mountains in eastern Oregon, northern Washington, Idaho, and British Columbia.

Location	Trend	Circles	Birds/100 ph
BC	0.1	15	0.13
WA	0.5	23	0.13
OR	-0.5	28	0.56
ALL	-0.7	1168	6.16

Grasshopper Sparrow
Ammodramus savannarum

The species has been recorded twice on the Eugene, OR, CBC near sites where it breeds in some years.

Fox Sparrow
Passerella iliaca

Most of the Fox Sparrows that breed in the region winter to the south, while large numbers of sparrows from more northerly locales move into the western part of the region. The species is abundant almost anywhere that there is dense undergrowth at low elevations west of the high Cascades. Hundreds can be found on coastal CBCs, and this species is one that inhabits recent overgrown clear-cuts in winter, using the dense shrub

growth along with Winter
Wrens, Wrentits, and other
species.

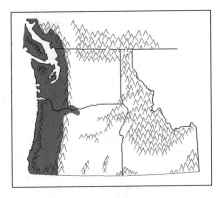

East of the Cascades these
sparrows are much harder to
find, occurring mainly in
dense lowland thickets. CBC
numbers are usually below
ten birds at most sites. Even
in the Klamath Basin the
species is hard to find and
often absent.

Fox Sparrows are usually absent from southern Idaho in
winter, but a few can sometimes be found in appropriate habitat
in the panhandle and in southwestern Idaho. It is a rare winter
lingerer in the Okanagan Valley, BC.

It is not clear why Oregon shows such an increase in CBC
numbers over time, but the advent of several new CBCs on the
coast since the mid-1980s added some of the best habitat for this
species and resulted in some very high counts per party hour,
possibly lifting the state trend figures.

Location	Trend	Circles	Birds/100 ph
BC	0.0	38	1.93
WA	0.5	33	2.07
OR	5.8	34	5.14
ALL	-0.2	1358	0.94

Song Sparrow
Melospiza melodia

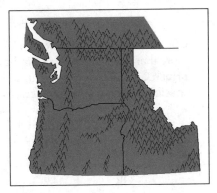

This is one of the birds that is
present throughout the
region in winter, occurring
wherever there is adequate
brushy cover below the snow
zone. Song Sparrows are
abundant west of the
Cascades and locally
common even in the higher,
colder parts of the region in

Location	Trend	Circles	Birds/100 ph
BC	-1.5	47	7.83
ID	-1.9	18	10.42
WA	0.7	36	16.06
OR	3.0	45	18.41
ALL	-0.4	1944	8.89

eastern Oregon, Idaho, eastern Washington, and British
Columbia.

Numbers east of the mountains vary from year to year,
perhaps dependent on the severity of the winter or the
availability of food. The species is almost always present in
small numbers even in years of severe conditions. However,
trend data suggest a possible long-term tendency away from
colder areas to more mild wintering grounds.

Lincoln's Sparrow
Melospiza lincolnii

These small grass-loving
sparrows can be locally
common west of the Cascades
in winter, but are usually rare
or absent east of the
mountains, although ten were
found during the 1995 CBC at
Summer Lake, OR, and small
numbers winter in
southwestern Idaho.

The species is most
common in Oregon, where
CBC tallies often exceed twenty birds and have exceeded forty
more than once. In western Washington and southwestern
British Columbia counts are usually under ten birds, and the
species is very rare in the interior valleys of British Columbia in

Location	Trend	Circles	Birds/100 ph
BC	1.1	16	0.04
WA	0.2	17	0.26
OR	4.9	28	0.16
ALL	-0.8	722	0.84

the winter. Birds can be found in any brushy area, but the species is partial to sites with such plants as canary grass, teasel, and thistle adjacent to dense cover such as blackberries. They often feed in the grass and shelter in the berry tangles. Several birds can sometimes be found together in these places.

These patches of "kack" are among the most productive winter birding sites in the Northwest. See Irons and Fix (1991) for a discussion of the species that use these areas and how to cover them.

Swamp Sparrow
Melospiza georgiana

Until the late 1960s this species was rarely reported in the Northwest, but today it is known to be an annual wintering bird. Along the Oregon coast it can be common very locally in preferred habitat; the only areas where ten or more birds can often be found are around Tillamook Bay and in the Coquille Valley. Elsewhere on the coast it is uncommon.

In the western interior valleys of Oregon it is occasional but is being found more often, perhaps because more observers are looking carefully in the boggy blackberry-canary grass-willow sumps that it prefers.

In western Washington it is being reported more often, and there are now winter records at several sites in eastern Oregon, southeast Washington, and Idaho. Although the number of birds east of the Cascades is small, records have come from widely diverse areas, including riparian areas at relatively high elevations. In southwestern British Columbia, the species is an increasing local winterer, and it is very rare in the interior valleys of British Columbia.

White-throated Sparrow
Zonotrichia albicollis

This species is uncommon west of the Cascades and occasional to rare east of the mountains. Numbers vary considerably from year to year, especially in BC, Washington, and east of the Cascades.

It is most common in western Oregon, where CBC numbers sometimes exceed ten birds. The species is annual at many CBCs, with numbers increasing southward. Portland averages one bird per year, Corvallis two, and Eugene four. CBC trend data show an increase in the coastal part of the region, especially in Oregon.

East of the Cascades single birds are the CBC norm but in some years multiple birds are reported, mainly from feeders and from lowland areas where large flocks of White-crowned Sparrows gather. Small numbers winter annually in southwest Idaho.

Location	Trend	Circles	Birds/100 ph
BC	0.3	14	0.03
WA	0.1	17	0.07
OR	3.7	29	2.35
ALL	-0.6	1638	10.27

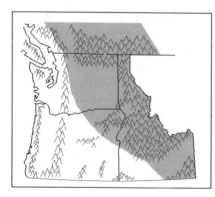

Harris's Sparrow
Zonotrichia querula

This species is rare but regular in winter in British Columbia, Washington, Idaho, and eastern Oregon. It is most often reported from inland British Columbia, southern Idaho, and northeastern Oregon, where birds sometimes appear with groups of White-crowned

Location	Trend	Circles	Birds/100 ph
BC	0.2	21	0.11
WA	-0.5	17	0.04
OR	-0.1	29	0.07
ALL	-2.2	595	5.61

Sparrows or juncos. Although numbers vary from year to year, a few birds are always present in winter in the eastern half of the region, and multiple birds can be found in some years. In the Okanagan Valley the species is found on about half of Vernon, BC, CBCs, with a record high of nine birds and an average of 1.5 birds. It is less frequent farther south in the valley. At American Falls, ID, the species has been found on about one-third of counts, and on about 40 percent at Pocatello, ID.

Farther south and west the species is found on about 20 percent of Spokane, WA, and Union County, OR, counts. Even farther southwest the species is much less common, rarely reaching the eastern foothills of the Oregon Cascades. The only area west of the Cascades where the species is nearly annual is the northern end of Puget Sound and southwestern British Columbia. The Bellingham, WA, CBC finds the species on 70 percent of counts.

It is rare in most of western Washington and western Oregon, where there are usually one or two birds every winter. The species is very rare in southwestern Oregon, rarely reaching the Rogue or Umpqua valleys or the southern Oregon coast.

White-crowned Sparrow
Zonotrichia leucophrys

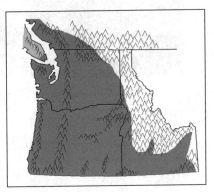

This species is one of the most widespread and locally abundant in the region in winter. Hundreds of birds can be found in favored areas of brushland throughout the region. The greatest concentrations are along the Columbia-Snake system and in the western interior valleys. Even at northerly locations such as Vernon, BC, the species is regular, averaging over ten birds per count.

White-crowned and White-throated Sparrows

Location	Trend	Circles	Birds/100 ph
BC	1.2	33	2.78
WA	-3.1	34	28.99
OR	1.5	42	12.49
ALL	-1.5	1530	24.82

West of the Cascades the species is most common on the outer coast and at inland sites where dense cover—often blackberry patches—can be found adjacent to semi-open country. It is much less common in areas that are primarily forest with only small openings. At preferred sites scores, even hundreds, of birds can often be found in a relatively small area.

East of the Cascades the species is somewhat more local, being locally abundant in brushy bottomlands along the Columbia-Snake system and major tributaries, but only occasional to uncommon at nearby sites without adequate habitat. It is locally abundant east as far as the eastern Snake River valley of Idaho.

Feeding groups often spread out from sheltering bushes onto nearby open ground such as pastures, feeding until flushed back to cover. This "tidal" feeding routine is quite pronounced in this species along with the Golden-crowned Sparrow, as distinguished from sparrows like the Song, Fox, and Lincoln's Sparrow that prefer to feed in or close to cover.

The races that winter in the Northwest are in part representative of birds that breed at more northerly locations. Birds of the *gambelii* race that winter mainly east of the Cascades breed in northwestern Canada and Alaska, while most of the birds west of the mountains are thought to be of the race *pugetensis*, which breeds along the Northwest coast to Alaska and also at some western montane sites.

Golden-crowned Sparrow
Zonotrichia atricapilla

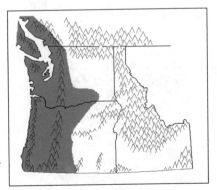

This is one of the most common winter sparrows in western Oregon and Washington and on Vancouver Island, with the greatest numbers found in dense lowland blackberry thickets and other shrubs. The species is common to uncommon in mainland southwestern British Columbia.

Location	Trend	Circles	Birds/100 ph
BC	1.9	26	0.88
WA	4.7	31	2.54
OR	0.4	33	11.36
ALL	-0.8	276	4.22

The greatest densities are in southwestern Oregon, where CBC numbers are often in the hundreds, though it is also common along the coast where adequate habitat exists. Eugene and Corvallis, OR, average about six hundred birds per count, while Medford, OR, averages 867. Puget Sound counts have lower averages, with fifty-three at Bellingham, WA, and Olympia, WA, and twenty-four at Seattle, WA. However, Washington shows the most distinct increase over the past thirty years.

East of the Cascades the species is occasional to rare, found mainly in lowland brushy areas with White-crowned Sparrows. In general, the farther east a CBC is located the fewer birds it finds. The species is occasional in lowlands from the Okanagan Valley (rare) south along the eastern edge of the Cascades, in the Summer Lake, OR, area (almost annual), and in the Columbia bottoms east to the Tri-Cities, WA (rare). It is very rare in winter as far east as the eastern tier of counties in Washington and Oregon, and in Idaho.

The only site east of the Cascades where the species is relatively common is in the Klamath Basin, where the CBC averages thirty-three birds per year.

Dark-eyed Junco
Junco hyemalis

Juncos are among the most abundant and ubiquitous winter birds in most of the region. They are absent from high elevations and dense forests, but can be found in brushy areas, towns, gardens, and fencerows almost anywhere else. The greatest

Dark-eyed Juncos

numbers can be found in the western interior valleys, where CBC numbers in the thousands are routine, but significant numbers remain in lowland areas east of the Cascades, especially in the Columbia-Snake valleys and the lake basins of south-central Oregon. Scores or hundreds of these birds can be found in these lowlands on CBCs. Hundreds are also usually found on CBCs in the Okanagan Valley north into British Columbia. Most of the juncos found in the region are "Oregon" juncos, but a few "Slate-colored" juncos are present throughout the region in most years.

The slight decrease noted regionwide could be the result of an actual population drop or an artifact of changes in CBC coverage. Juncos are reported in abundance from many long-standing counts in towns and small cities, some of which generate high party-hour totals in areas full of juncos. Many of the newer counts in the region are on the outer coast or east of the Cascades, where juncos are more patchy in distribution,

Location	Trend	Circles	Birds/100 ph
BC	-2.4	47	31.87
ID	-3.3	17	31.43
WA	-0.1	36	84.73
OR	-1.7	45	82.11
ALL	-1.3	2035	41.25

there are fewer yards with feeders, and observers are more focused on water birds and raptors. Adding a lot of new party hours over several years while not adding a lot of junco territory would have the effect of creating an artificial population drop.

McCown's Longspur
Calcarius mccownii

This bird is rare in winter in the Klamath Basin. Two records have been accepted by the OBRC. A male was found in southern Klamath County, OR, on January 31, 1981. Another male was at Lower Klamath NWR, Klamath County, OR, from January 13 to 15, 1990. Two were at Atomic City, ID, on February 20, 1980 (Taylor and Trost 1987).

Lapland Longspur
Calcarius lapponicus

Although this species has been found at a variety of locations in the region in winter, it is not regular anywhere except in the Klamath Basin and locally in western and central Washington, where it is uncommon to occasional. Away from the Klamath Basin most records are from southeastern Idaho, northern Puget Sound, the outer coast of Washington and the open plateaus of central and southeastern Washington. Although the species is found almost every year on the Bellingham, WA, and Grays Harbor, WA, CBCs, it is much rarer on the Oregon coast, where the well-covered Tillamook Bay CBC has never found the species in thirty-one years, and Yaquina Bay only once in twenty-two years.

The species is very rare in winter in the western interior valleys and the Okanagan Valley, BC.

Small flocks of these birds are sometimes found alone or with Snow Buntings, Horned Larks, or American Pipits.

Chestnut-collared Longspur
Calcarius ornatus

A vagrant. One was on the 1989 Moscow, ID-Pullman, WA, CBC.

Rustic Bunting
Emberiza rustica

A vagrant. One was at the Kent sewage ponds, King County, WA, from December 15, 1986 through March 22, 1987, and another, believed to be the same bird, was at the same locale from December 11, 1988, through April 1989 (Tweit and Skriletz 1996).

Snow Bunting
Plectrophenax nivalis

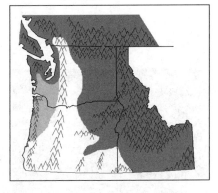

This species is locally common in the eastern and northwestern part of the region and is progressively less common farther south and west. Although the number of birds present varies considerably from year to year, scores can often be found in northeastern Oregon (especially Wallowa County), southern Idaho, and northeastern and north coastal Washington. Large flocks can be found in the plateau country of central and southeastern Washington. It is rare in winter in the Okanagan Valley, west to the Cascades and the Willamette valley and south to the basins of south-central Oregon. It is extremely rare to southwestern Oregon.

It is also regular on the outer coast south to northwestern Oregon. The Grays Harbor, WA, and Tillamook Bay, OR, CBCs find it, sometimes in numbers, on about 25 percent of counts.

Location	Trend	Circles	Birds/100 ph
BC	-3.8	26	4.52
ALL	-2.1	1054	83.41

South of Tillamook Bay it is distinctly less common, with a few birds appearing at Newport, OR, in some years and no regular appearances farther south.

This species is locally common on the northern coast of Puget Sound and north to coastal southwestern British Columbia. It is found on almost all Bellingham, WA, CBCs, where the average annual count is close to 17 birds.

McKay's Bunting
Plectrophenax hyperboreus

This bird is a vagrant from Alaska. There are two records of three birds for Washington; two birds from December 1978 through March 1979, and one from January 15 to April 1, 1988, all at Ocean Shores, Grays Harbor County. Oregon's sole record was of two birds at the south jetty of the Columbia River from February 23 to March 2, 1980.

Family Cardinalidae

Rose-breasted Grosbeak

Woahink Lake, OR, December 13, 1989
Photograph by Bill Stotz

Rose-breasted Grosbeak
Pheucticus ludovicianus

This is a rare vagrant in winter. There are three winter records for Oregon, all photographed. One was at Lake Oswego, Clackamas County, on December 25, 1972. Another was at Woahink Lake, Lane County, on December 13, 1989. The third was December 15, 1995, at Hunter Creek, Curry County. One was at Mountain Home, ID, December 2, 1983 (*American Birds* 38(3): 339). Another was at Chehalis, Lewis County, WA, from January 13 to 16, 1990 (Tweit and Skriletz 1996).

Black-headed Grosbeak
Pheucticus melanocephalus

This species is extremely rare in winter. The three reported on the 1967 Medford, OR, CBC are probably in error. One was at a feeder in Scappoose, Columbia County, OR, in winter 1995.

Blue Grosbeak
Guiraca caerulea

This is a rare vagrant. There are two winter records from Oregon, one photographed at Corvallis, Benton County, on January 4+, 1975, and one east of Fern Ridge Reservoir, Lane County, on December 21, 1980. These constituted the only accepted records for Oregon until a pair bred in northern Malheur County in 1997.

Indigo Bunting
Passerina cyanea

A rare vagrant. One was found with sparrows in a park in Eugene, OR, from November 29 to December 4, 1975.

Dickcissel
Spiza americana

A vagrant to the region in winter. Three records have been accepted by the OBRC. One was at Lakeside, Coos County, from November 30 to December 1, 1979. Another was at Astoria, Clatsop County, from December 10, 1988, to January 19, 1989. One was at Manzanita, Tillamook County, on 19 February 19, 1986.

One was at Ocean Shores, WA, on February 18, 1996. Another was at Puget Island, Wahkiakum County, WA, from December 23, 1983, through April 14, 1984 (Tweit and Skriletz 1996).

Dickcissel

Lakeside, OR, December 1, 1979
(Photograph by Owen Schmidt)

Family Icteridae

Bobolink
Dolichonyx oryzivorus

A rare lingerer. Two birds at Myrtle Point, Coos County, OR, on December 10, 1979, are the only winter reports for the region.

Red-winged Blackbird
Agelaius phoeniceus

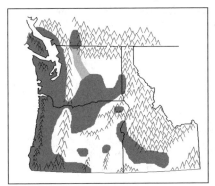

The Red-winged Blackbird is locally abundant where large flocks form in winter. The largest numbers can be found in the western interior valleys and locally along the Columbia-Snake system where foraging areas are nearby.

East of the Cascades this species can be hard to find away from lowland flocking areas, but some remain, especially where there is access to feed grain such as in cattle feedlots and towns.

In the western interior valleys the species can be abundant, especially where major roosts form, such as the several thousand that usually winter at Fern Ridge Reservoir, Lane County, OR.

In coastal areas the species can be hard to find, with most birds gathering around feedlots and other sources of food. Because of its winter feeding preferences it is found mainly along parts of the coast with significant dairy herds.

The species is absent from most marsh areas at higher elevations, but some gather at lowland marshes such as the

Location	Trend	Circles	Birds/100 ph
ID	3.1	15	72.99
WA	-0.4	34	38.36
OR	5.7	42	36.39
BC	1.7	36	13.75
ALL	1.6	1877	2302.01

Potholes region of central Washington, Summer Lake, OR, and in the Klamath Basin. Because of the tendency of the species to form large flocks in winter, the reliability of CBC data is colored by the perennial question of whether the largest local flock was in or out of the count circle on count day.

Tricolored Blackbird
Agelaius tricolor

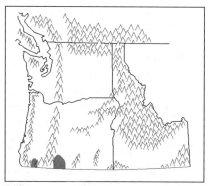

This species is very local and usually uncommon, with most birds found in the Klamath Basin and in the eastern Rogue Valley. The Klamath Falls, OR, CBC averages about one hundred birds; smaller numbers are usually found in the Rogue Valley. A few can sometimes be found elsewhere in central Oregon.

The species has been found breeding locally north to Portland and Umatilla County, OR, in recent years, so it is possible that a few Tricolored Blackbirds have remained undetected in winter in Red-winged Blackbird flocks.

Western Meadowlark
Sturnella neglecta

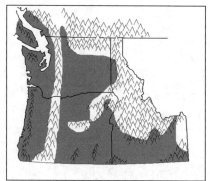

This species is locally common throughout the region in overgrown fields, grasslands, and sagebrush, mainly at lower elevations. Birds can also be found in dune grass along the coast. Wintering numbers have slowly dwindled in the past thirty years, with the continental drop exceeded by regional decreases, particularly in British Columbia. This decrease matches decreases in the breeding population in some areas. This species has been adversely affected by habitat loss in many agricultural areas.

Location	Trend	Circles	Birds/100 ph
BC	-6.7	24	0.8
WA	-2.7	30	4.29
OR	-0.2	36	8.83
ALL	-1.4	723	17.59

West of the Cascades this species is common in flocks where there are open, overgrown grassy areas in which to feed. Meadowlarks are sometimes found feeding with flocks of starlings and blackbirds in winter, but often they form flocks solely with other meadowlarks. The species is generally less common on the coast, where it can be hard to find.

Although many birds leave the higher-elevation sage deserts, cultivated areas, and grasslands east of the Cascades, some remain, especially in the Columbia-Snake valleys and the lake basins of south-central Oregon. These birds sometimes flock with other icterids and can be found around feedlots and other food sources. Some winter north to the Okanagan Valley but numbers there are believed to be declining according to Cannings et al. (1987). The species is local in winter in southern Idaho.

Yellow-headed Blackbird
Xanthocephalus
xanthocephalus

This species appears to be increasing in winter in the region. It is annual in small numbers in the Klamath Basin and occasional at Summer Lake, Lake County, OR. It is also being reported more often north to central Washington and in southern Idaho in winter, and small numbers can be found in the Okanagan Valley, BC, and around Vancouver, BC, in some years. The reasons for this trend are not clear. Numbers are usually small, but several hundred birds were in the Moses Lake, WA, area in the winter of 1993-94 and 1994-95, and small flocks are often noted in the Klamath Basin.

There are occasional reports of birds west of the Cascades.

Rusty Blackbird
Euphagus carolinus

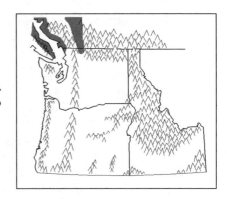

This species is occasional in winter in British Columbia, both inland and on the coast. It is rare but regular in Idaho (most regular at St. Maries) and Washington (most consistently found in northern Puget Sound and the Walla Walla areas), and rare in Oregon. There are three winter records for Oregon and one winter record for the Pocatello, ID, CBC.

Brewer's Blackbird
Euphagus cyanocephalus

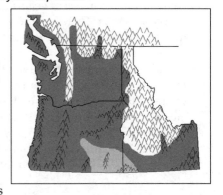

This blackbird can be found throughout the region in winter, but concentrates in lowlands and towns. Like the Red-winged Blackbird, it also forms flocks (often mixed with other species) in winter, but small numbers of birds can be found away from concentration areas, especially in towns, where they often forage along streets and in parks.

The bulk of birds that breed at higher elevations and more northerly latitudes away from the coast leave in winter, moving south and down into warmer lowland areas. The species can be common to abundant in the western interior valleys, along Puget Sound, and locally in the Columbia lowlands east to the Tri-Cities, WA, area. It is uncommon to rare elsewhere east of the Cascades in winter, with remaining birds flocking in areas with available food such as feedlots.

This species is often hard to find on the outer coast in winter except in areas with cattle feedlots or other concentrated food sources.

Location	Trend	Circles	Birds/100 ph
BC	-5.6	36	20.76
ID	-4.4	16	54.63
WA	-3.9	34	56.82
OR	-2.0	44	103.33
ALL	-1.1	1013	141.00

The reasons for the apparent regionwide winter population decrease are not clear. It may be that the effect of many new CBCs starting in the 1970s and 1980s in areas where the species is not common has colored the data. The species continues to be a common, locally abundant breeder in the region.

Common Grackle
Quiscalus quiscula

This species is rare in winter in southeastern Idaho. It has colonized Idaho in recent years and birds now occasionally stay into early winter. There are also at least two winter records for the Idaho panhandle. One was in Salmon on December 26, 1984 (Roberts 1992).

There is a single winter record from Oregon, one that spent the winter of 1996-97 near Tumalo, Deschutes County. One wintered in Revelstoke, BC, in the winter of 1989-90, and there are two winter records from Washington, one at College Place, Walla Walla County, from January 1 to 6, 1995, and one at Olympia, Thurston County, from December 4, 1974, through January 18, 1975 (Tweit and Skriletz 1996).

Great-tailed Grackle
Quiscalus mexicanus

There are several winter records in Idaho, at Burley, Marsing, and American Falls. A high count of eight was reported west of Pocatello, ID, during the 1995 CBC. One adult female was at Vernon, BC, from December 5, 1993 until March 1994.

Brown-headed Cowbird
Molothrus ater

Although most cowbirds leave the Northwest in winter, some remain, almost exclusively with blackbird flocks. The species is most often reported in the western interior valleys, in dairy farming areas along the coast, and locally along the Columbia River and in the Klamath Basin. Away from these areas, where the species is found as an occasional component of large blackbird flocks, it is rare. East of the Cascades it is very local, absent in some years, and rare in any year to far eastern British Columbia, Oregon, Washington, and all of Idaho, although it is regularly found around feedlots in south-central Idaho. The species is very rare north to the Okanagan Valley in winter, with three records cited by Cannings et al., all from cattle feedlots.

Location	Trend	Circles	Birds/100 ph
WA	-3.3	23	1.39
OR	0.2	30	1.00
ALL	-2.1	1626	330.93

Orchard Oriole
Icterus spurius

There is one recent winter record for Washington on Samish Island, Skagit County, from December 15 to 27, 1991. One was at Brookings, Curry County, OR, from November 12 to December 12, 1990, and was accepted by the OBRC.

Hooded Oriole
Icterus cucullatus

This rare wanderer from California and the southwest sometimes moves northward in winter to visit the Northwest. One was at Depoe Bay, Lincoln County, OR, on December 9-

Hooded Oriole

Coos Bay, OR, December 1982
(Photograph by Barbara S. Griffin)

29+, 1976. Another was in Eugene, Lane County, OR, from January 1 through March 1979. One was in Coos Bay, Coos County, OR, on December 16+, 1979, and two were present there in the winter of 1982-83, with one bird found on December 24, 1982, and another seen February 2 to 19, 1983. Most of these birds were photographed and all have been accepted by the OBRC.

Baltimore Oriole
Icterus galbula

A vagrant. One was at Brookings, Curry County, OR, from December 1, 1991, through March 7, 1992.

Bullock's Oriole
Icterus bullocki

Bullock's Oriole

Mt. Vernon, WA, February 1993
(Photograph by Mike Denny)

Most orioles leave the Northwest in winter, but there are a number of records of birds that remained at least into early winter, often at suet or hummingbird feeders. There are two winter records for the Okanagan Valley, the latter of which was photographed as it regularly attended a suet feeder. One bird visited a Kelowna, BC, feeder from December 1991 to February 1992.

There are two confirmed Washington winter records of which I am aware, a male at Mt. Vernon from January to February 1993, and another on December 16, 1995, at Ocean Shores, Grays Harbor County. There are at least four additional winter records from Washington (Phil Mattocks, personal communication).

According to Gilligan et al. (1994) there are about thirteen winter records of Bullock's Oriole in Oregon. Documentation for most of these records is not available, but it appears that the species does occasionally remain into early winter, especially in the southwestern part of the state. There is one winter record for Baker County, OR.

One early-winter record in the Idaho panhandle was at Sandpoint on December 16, 1989.

Scott's Oriole
Icterus parisorum

This bird is a rare vagrant from the southwest. One adult male came to a bird feeder at Chehalis, Lewis County, WA, from February 11 to April 13, 1980.

Family Fringillidae
Subfamily Fringillinae

Brambling
Fringilla montifringilla

This vagrant from Siberia is rare in the Northwest but has occurred several times at widely scattered locations. There are several records from northern British Columbia, where the species is almost annual now. Southern British Columbia records include a female at Vancouver on January 6, 1991, and single females in the winter 1991/92 at Alaksen NWA, Delta; Nelson, West Kootenays; and Westham Island, Ladner.

There are at least eight winter records for Washington (Tweit and Skriletz 1996), four from the minor invasion of winters 1990-91 and 1991-92. Oregon has five winter records of this species. The first record for the lower forty-eight states was at Portland, OR, from November 22, 1967, through March 31, 1968. There are no records for Idaho.

Brambling
———————
Naselle, WA, December 1995
(Photograph by Ruth Sullivan)

Subfamily Carduelinae

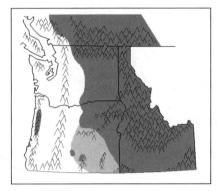

Gray-crowned Rosy-Finch
Leucosticte tephrocotis

This species forms flocks in winter and can be abundant—or absent—in the open fields and grassy hillsides of southern British Columbia (locally), eastern Washington, north-central to southeastern Oregon, and Idaho. Because flocks are sometimes huge, exceeding a thousand birds, the species can be absent from large expanses of territory yet abundant just over the next ridge.

Two well-marked subspecies can be found in the region. The gray-hooded "Hepburn's" form breeds in the Cascades and in the coastal mountains of British Columbia, and most winter nearby. This is the form found throughout Washington. In Idaho and eastern Oregon the form with a smaller gray cap is seen more often.

Count	% of counts
Penticton, BC	29
Moscow, ID-Pullman, WA	46
Union County, OR	54
Baker, OR	37
Pocatello, ID	45

These birds are most often found along the eastern edge of the region, where they are common in the open wheat fields and grasslands adjacent to the montane areas where they breed. They also winter in canyon areas, where Cliff Swallow nests are often used for roosting. They also occur in the smaller intermontane valleys of eastern Idaho.

West of the Cascades the species is rare in most places but occasional to uncommon at preferred sites such as the top of Mary's Peak in the coast range of Benton County, OR, where a few can be found in most winters. It is rare to the floor of the western interior valleys and very rare to the coast.

Location	Trend	Circles	Birds/100 ph
BC	-4.6	17	1.82
ALL	-3.2	149	15.37

Black Rosy-Finch
Leucosticte atratus

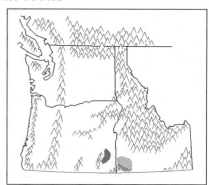

This species has been reported in winter along the edge of the Alvord Desert in Harney County, OR, adjacent to Steens Mountain where a small population breeds. There are a few reports of this species mixed in with large flocks of Gray-crowned Rosy Finches to northeastern Oregon and southwestern Idaho. It is rare in the Pocatello area of southeastern Idaho.

Pine Grosbeak
Pinicola enucleator

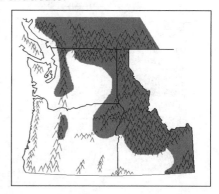

Although the trend data do not include Idaho, presumably because few counts are held there, this is the part of the region where Pine Grosbeaks are most regular and common in winter, along with northeastern Oregon, far eastern Washington, and eastern British Columbia.

This big finch stays fairly close to its breeding areas in winter, moving downslope but not far away. For this reason it is rare in western Oregon and Washington but fairly easy to find in some years in the lowlands along the Rocky Mountains. Farther west it is much less regular, probably because the breeding population in the

Location	Trend	Circles	Birds/100 ph
BC	-4.9	37	5.12
WA	-2.0	17	2.21
ALL	0.8	840	4.41

Count	% of counts
Campbell River, BC	14
Vernon, BC	75
Bellingham, WA	23
Spokane, WA	40
Union County, OR	46
Baker, OR	37
Indian Mountain, ID	40
Pocatello, ID	41

western fringes of the Blue Mountains and in the Oregon and southern Washington Cascades is small.

In northwestern Washington near Bellingham and in mainland southwestern British Columbia the species is occasional in the lowlands in winter, probably because these areas are adjacent to montane locales where the species breeds. Elsewhere west of the Cascades the species is rare, but a few birds are reported from lowland areas and occasionally from the coast range in winter.

Purple Finch
Carpodacus purpureus

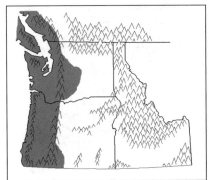

This species is locally common from the Cascades westward. CBC numbers vary from a few birds to more than a hundred and the species can be found at most westside counts.

A few birds can be found on the eastern slopes of the Cascades, especially in the Klamath Basin and in Kittitas and Chelan counties, WA, but the species is rare in the lowlands and farther east and very rare to far eastern Oregon and Washington and in Idaho.

Location	Trend	Circles	Birds/100 ph
BC	-0.7	29	2.52
WA	-2.5	31	3.70
OR	-0.5	32	2.91
ALL	0.6	1661	2.68

Cassin's Finch
Carpodacus cassinii

This is the common finch of coniferous forests from the Cascade summit eastward; it is common in pine habitats throughout the eastern part of the region. Some descend to the lowlands in winter. Most leave interior British Columbia and central Washington in winter except in years of heavy ponderosa pine cone crops.

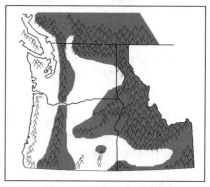

Although the species is reported fairly often on CBCs west of the Cascades, many reports cannot be confirmed. However, it is clear that a few birds do come down the west side of the Cascades in winter in some years. This may be especially true in southwestern Oregon where significant stands of pine can be found on the west side of the Cascade ridges and in the Siskiyou range.

Location	Trend	Circles	Birds/100 ph
OR	-0.3	21	1.55
ALL	-2.2	242	2.46

House Finch
Carpodacus mexicanus

This is the most widespread finch in the region, remaining even in colder areas through the winter. It is common to abundant in most areas except for montane forests and open range, and often forms small flocks in fall and winter. House Finches can be found around farm buildings, in towns, in hedgerows and blackberry patches, and even

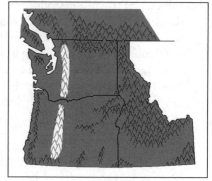

Location	Trend	Circles	Birds/100 ph
BC	-0.6	32	23.36
ID	6.6	14	20.47
WA	1.7	34	45.59
OR	2.1	43	26.85
ALL	0.5	1239	20.01

in dune grass, where they surprise many an observer hoping to find longspurs. CBC numbers range from a few at counts in heavily wooded areas to hundreds at locations with plenty of food sources in semi-open country or in towns.

At the northern edge of their range in central British Columbia they are found mainly around human habitation and are seriously depleted by harsh winters.

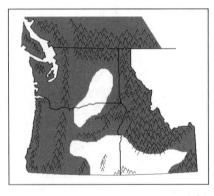

Red Crossbill
Loxia curvirostra

This locally abundant mountain finch often moves into lowlands throughout the wooded parts of the region in winter. Numbers vary considerably from year to year.

This species is most common in the region's coniferous forests, but downslope movements that often begin in late summer sometimes bring thousands of birds into lowland areas and to the coast. Although they reach most of the region in winter, very few occur to southern Idaho, southeastern Oregon, and the open country of the Columbia basin.

Numbers in the western interior valleys are usually lower than numbers found in either the Cascades or the coast ranges. The species is absent from lowland areas in some years.

Location	Trend	Circles	Birds/100 ph
BC	2.0	40	6.79
WA	4.1	25	7.07
OR	1.1	28	2.53
ALL	0.5	932	2.07

This species' breeding cycle is linked more to available food (good cone seed crops) than to season of the year; breeding often occurs in mid-winter when conditions permit.

White-winged Crossbill
Loxia leucoptera

This species is irregular and occasional from northern Idaho west to south-central British Columbia, south rarely as far as central Washington and the central Cascades of Oregon.

Numbers on the region's CBCs even in British Columbia are usually small, although invasion years have brought several hundred to the Okanagan Valley and scores into the Idaho panhandle and northeastern Washington. Only in peak invasion years does the species reach western Washington, southern Idaho, or any locations in Oregon in numbers.

The relative scarcity of this species even on the region's more northerly CBCs may stem from its preference for spruce cones rather than the Douglas-fir and pine seeds often used by Red Crossbills, according to Cannings et al. (1987). Birds that enter the region in winter may remain at elevations higher than the sites normally visited by observers.

Location	Trend	Circles	Birds/100 ph
BC	0.9	22	1.23
WA	-1.8	14	0.26
ALL	-0.8	667	3.58

Common Redpoll
Carduelis flammea

This small northern finch is common in winter in most years in the northern and northeastern part of the region. It generally arrives in numbers later in the season than many wintering species—often not until January in the southern parts of its

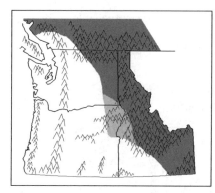

range—and as a consequence its actual abundance may not be accurately reflected in the region's CBC results, especially those counts in Oregon and southern Idaho.

Although numbers of this species vary from year to year, small flocks can be found annually from the Okanagan Valley south to north-central Washington. Birds are usually present in small numbers but sometimes in the low hundreds on northern Idaho CBCs and along the eastern edge of Washington. In some years flocks reach the open valleys in the Blue Mountains of northeastern Oregon and open country of southern Idaho.

Count	% of counts
Vaseux Lake, BC	76
Bellingham, WA	27
Spokane, WA	60
Moscow, ID-Pullman, WA	50
Baker, OR	17
Sandpoint, ID	67
Pocatello, ID	36

Farther south and west the species' numbers drop off dramatically. It is usually absent south of Wenatchee, WA, and west of the Blue Mountains in Oregon and southeastern Washington. In southern Idaho it is more regular in the eastern part of the state than in the open lowlands of the western Snake River plain. It is rare in Oregon south of the Blue Mountains but in peak years a few birds reach the east side of the Cascades. There are a few records for western Oregon south and west to Florence, Lane County, but the species is very rare on the west side.

The species is occasional in coastal western British Columbia and in Washington south to Bellingham, but rare as far south as Seattle and in the southwestern part of the state. Birds at the edge of their range are often found with flocks of goldfinches foraging in open country along hedgerows or in catkin-bearing trees.

Location	Trend	Circles	Birds/100 ph
BC	8.6	30	14.36
WA	-0.5	14	5.35
ALL	-0.5	1045	20.49

Hoary Redpoll
Carduelis hornemanni

This species is considered by some to be conspecific with the Common Redpoll. It is rare east of the Cascades in southern British Columbia, northeastern Washington, and northern Idaho.

In Washington there are only three reports accepted by the Records Committee, all in January in Okanogan County. A report of a bird at Marietta, Whatcom County, on December 28, 1969 (*AFN* 24:532) has been voted down by the Records Committee (Mattocks and Aanerud 1997). One generally accepted but unreviewed record was at Chewelah during the peak year of 1977.

It is very rare in Idaho. One was at Nampa in December 1977 during an invasion year (*American Birds* 32(3): 379), and two were at Moscow in the winter 1995/96.

It is essentially a vagrant to Oregon, with records of one to three birds near Umapine, Milton-Freewater, and Weston, Umatilla County, on January 21 and February 1, 2 and 5, 1986. The only other record for the state was of a bird 9 miles northwest of Bates, Grant County, on January 19, 1990.

Pine Siskin
Carduelis pinus

This small arboreal finch occurs in wooded areas throughout the region in winter. It is most common from the Cascades westward and along the foothills of the Rockies. It is present in smaller numbers along the east side of the Cascades, in the Blue Mountain region, and at more isolated wooded locations such as towns and 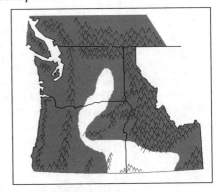 riparian areas in the Columbia Basin and Great Basin.

It often forms huge flocks in winter, descending into the lowlands and foothill forests by the hundreds. Flocks in excess of two thousand birds have been seen on occasion in the coast ranges in winter, but smaller groups of a few dozen to a hundred are more normal.

Location	Trend	Circles	Birds/100 ph
BC	2.5	44	53.89
ID	3.1	17	54.47
WA	-1.5	34	25.90
OR	3.0	41	14.80
ALL	2.2	1823	11.67

Numbers vary widely from year to year. In some years birds remain at higher elevations in the Cascades, Rockies, and other ranges where CBCs are not held, thereby remaining untallied, but most years bring significant numbers into the foothills and valleys. In some years these birds are very common at feeders in urban areas.

Lesser Goldfinch
Carduelis psaltria

In Oregon, this species is abundant in the Rogue Valley and common north to the southern Willamette Valley. Numbers decrease northward through the Willamette Valley and it is occasional at Portland. It is occasional on the southern Oregon coast and rare to absent north of Coos County.

Count (all OR)	% of counts
Portland	67
Corvallis	70
Eugene	100
Medford	100
Klamath Falls	82

Location	Trend	Circles	Birds/100 ph
OR	4.3	15	8.82
ALL	-1.5	303	5.45

East of the Cascades it is common in the Klamath Basin and occasional elsewhere in south-central Oregon east to the southern Warner Valley, although in severe winters most birds withdraw southward. It is rare in winter north to Crook County. A few birds are resident at Lyle, WA, at the eastern end of the Columbia River gorge.

Lawrence's Goldfinch
Carduelis lawrencei

A vagrant. A male was photographed at a feeder in Florence, Lane County, OR, from December 24, 1991, to January 11, 1992. This is the only winter record for the region.

Lawrence's Goldfinch

*Florence, OR, December 1991
(Photograph by Bill Stotz)*

American Goldfinch
Carduelis tristis

This is a common species in much of the region in lowland hedgerows, brushy areas, and riparian areas. It is common to abundant in the western interior valleys, throughout the Puget Sound lowlands and coastal southwestern British Columbia, and in most of the Columbia-Snake valleys. It is least common in the most

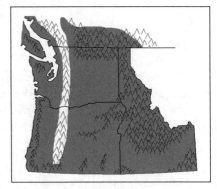

open areas of southeastern Oregon and on the outer coast. Numbers are smaller in northern Washington and British Columbia but many birds are still present.

CBC numbers vary from year to year, especially east of the Cascades. This may be due in part to some birds leaving in winter and others forming flocks that are not found on count

Location	Trend	Circles	Birds/100 ph
OR	3.2	43	10.78
WA	2.0	33	11.38
ID	-1.6	17	13.08
BC	4.1	29	5.03
ALL	1.6	1967	15.45

days. There is a general upward trend in the winter population from CBC data.

Evening Grosbeak
Coccothraustes vespertinus

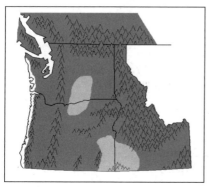

This large montane finch is common in much of the forested part of the region in winter, but is usually absent on the outer coast. It sometimes moves downslope in numbers in winter, but many birds remain in the mountains and foothills. Like most of the finches that breed in the high-elevation coniferous forests, numbers of this species in the lowlands in winter vary considerably from year to year, with hundreds of birds present one year and few or none the next year.

In most years the species is uncommon to occasional in the Rogue Valley lowlands. It is also hard to find in most years on the coastal slope of the coast ranges. The reasons for the general upward population trend are not clear.

Location	Trend	Circles	Birds/100 ph
BC	3.8	41	16.67
ID	9.6	15	34.61
WA	1.8	31	5.27
OR	3.1	44	5.62
ALL	3.2	1573	12.13

Family Passeridae

House Sparrow
Passer domesticus

This introduced species is abundant in urban areas and in rural areas where food, mainly grain, is available. CBC numbers probably reflect minimal abundance as most observers do not go out of their way to locate this ubiquitous bird. Despite its reputation as a widespread pest, this species is absent from forested areas and open desert except around habitations, and is not especially common on the coast (away from towns and dairy operations) compared to inland sites.

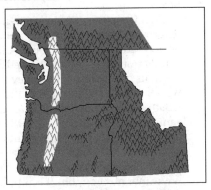

Location	Trend	Circles	Birds/100 ph
BC	-5.1	40	25.02
ID	-4.3	19	198.04
WA	-3.7	36	106.63
OR	0.6	45	53.49
ALL	-1.9	2107	290.44

Appendix

This is a portion of the text (modified slightly) provided by the U.S. Biological Service to accompany the data in the CBC trend boxes.

Trends are the population trends of North American birds as determined from analyses of data from the National Audubon Society Christmas Bird Count (CBC). They were analyzed using counts from the lower 48 United States and the southern portions of Canada. The survey time period was from the winter of 1959/60 through to the winter of 1988/89. See Butcher (1990) and Butcher and McCulloch (1990) for details on the sampling methodologies and biases associated with the CBC. To appear in this list, the species must have been seen at least once on more than 39 circles.

For CBC data via the World Wide Web see http:// www.mbr.nbs.gov/bbs/cbc.html.

Similar trend data (1966-1991) for the summertime are available for Breeding Bird Survey (BBS) data.

Interpreting Your Trend Data

Christmas Bird Counts were not designed to be a statistical sample of North American birds or their trends. Consequently, the locations are biased by the preferences of bird watchers as to where they would like to count birds. Often this translates to a bias toward urban areas and regions with high avian diversity. Interpretation of trends from such counts must be tempered by their inherent biases.

At this point we have not quantified the geographic or observer bias associated with CBCs. However, we did run a series of correlational analyses with data from the BBS. The BBS is not bias free, but does have an inherently better sampling scheme. Correlations between the two surveys do not necessarily prove that either program is truly tracking the population trends of any group of birds. However, high positive correlations between these two independent measures of bird population change strengthens the notion that both programs are appropriate measures of change. Indeed, when we ran those analyses we found highly significant positive correlations, especially in trends of permanent residents.

Literature Cited

Bellrose, F. 1976. Ducks, geese and swans of North America. Stackpole.

Bock, C. and T. Root. 1981. The Christmas Bird Count and avian ecology. Pages 17-23 *in* Estimating Numbers of Terrestrial Birds, Studies in Avian Biology No. 6, Cooper Ornithological Society.

Bond, C. 1987. Oregon's first Lucy's Warbler. *Oregon Birds* 13(3): 292.

Burleigh, T. 1957. Unusual early winter bird records from Oregon. *Condor* 59: 209.

Burleigh, T. 1970. Birds of Idaho. Caxton.

Butcher, G. S. 1990. Audubon Christmas Bird Counts. Pp. 5-13 in J. R. Sauer and S. Droege, eds., Survey designs and statistical methods for the estimation of avian population trends. U. S. Fish Wildl. Serv. Biol. Rep. 90(1).

Butcher, G. S. , and C. E. McCulloch. 1990. The influence of observer effort on the number of individual birds recorded on Christmas Bird Counts. Pp. 120-129 in Sauer, J. R. and S. Droege, eds. Survey designs and statistical methods for the estimation of avian population trends. U.S. Fish Wildl. Serv. Biol. Rep. 90(1).

Campbell, R., N. Dawe, J. Cooper, G. Kaiser, M. McNall, and I. McT. Cowan. 1990. Birds of British Columbia. Volumes 1 and 2. Royal British Columbia Museum.

Cannings, R. A., R. J. Cannings and S. G. Cannings. 1987. Birds of the Okanagan Valley, British Columbia. Royal British Columbia Museum.

Confer, J., T. Kaaret and L. Jones. 1979. Effort, Location and the Christmas Bird Count tally. *American Birds* 33(4): 690.

Contreras, A. 1986. The Art of the Christmas Bird Count. *Oregon Birds* 12(3) 192.

Contreras, A. 1992. Winter status of the Sora in the Pacific Northwest. *Western Birds* 23:137-142.

Contreras, A. and R. Kindschy. 1996. Birds of Malheur County, Oregon. Oregon Field Ornithologists Special Publication Number 8.

Drennan, S. 1981. The Christmas Bird Count: an overlooked and underused sample. Pages 24-29 *in* Estimating Numbers of Terrestrial Birds, Studies in Avian Biology No. 6, Cooper Ornithological Society.

Ehrlich, P., D. Dobkin and D. Wheye. 1988. The Birder's Handbook. Simon and Schuster.

Ennor, H. 1991. Birds of the Tri-Cities and Vicinity. Lower Columbia Basin Audubon Society.

Evanich, J. 1992. Birds of Northeast Oregon. Oregon Field Ornithologists Special Publication Number 6.

Falk, L. 1979. An examination of observers' weather sensitivity in Christmas Bird Count data. *American Birds* 33(4): 688.

Fix, D. 1987. A Record of 48 Western Screech-Owls on the Florence CBC. *Oregon Birds* 13(3): 278

Fix, D. 1988. Bird-finding Technique: Scanning the Sky. *Oregon Birds* 14(3): 247.

Fix, D. 1991. Birds of Diamond Lake Ranger District. Unpublished annotated list for the s. Oregon Cascades.

Fix, D. 1992. Notes on Observing Swamp Sparrows. *Oregon Birds* 18(4): 103.

Gabrielson, I. and S. Jewett. 1940. Birds of Oregon. Oregon State College.

Gilligan, J., Smith, M., Rogers, D. and Contreras, A. 1994. Birds of Oregon: status and distribution. Cinclus.

Goggans, R. and M. Platt. 1992. Breeding season observations of Great Gray Owls on the Willamette National Forest, Oregon. *Oregon Birds* 18: 35-41.

Harris, S. 1996. Northwestern California Birds. Second edition. Humboldt State University Press.

Henny, C., and G. Brady. 1994. Partial migration and wintering localities of American kestrels nesting in the Pacific Northwest. *Northwestern Naturalist* 75: 37.

Irons, D. and D. Fix. 1990. How to search for passerines more effectively in winter: notes on winter habitat microsites. *Oregon Birds* 16(4): 251

Jewett, S., Taylor, W., Shaw, W. and Aldrich, J. 1953. Birds of Washington State. University of Washington Press.

King, W., ed. 1974. Pelagic studies of seabirds in the central and eastern Pacific Ocean. Smithsonian Contributions to Zoology No. 158.

Larrison, E. and K. Sonnenberg. 1968. Washington Birds: their location and identification. Seattle Audubon Society.

Littlefield, C. 1990. Birds of Malheur National Wildlife Refuge. Oregon State University Press.

Madge, S. and H. Burn. 1988. Waterfowl: an identification guide to the ducks, geese and swans of the world. Houghton Mifflin.

Mattocks, P., Hunn, E., and Wahl, T. 1976. A checklist of the birds of Washington State, with recent changes annotated. *Western Birds* 7: 1.

Mattocks, P. and K. Aanerud. 1997. Second summary report of the Washington Bird Records Committee. *WOSNews* 47, p. 6. Washington Ornithological Society.

Nelson, J. 1947. Oystercatcher taken in Yakima County, Washington. *Murrelet* 28: 6.

Paulson, D. and P. Mattocks. 1992. Eastern Phoebes in Washington. *Washington Birds* 2: 20.

Paulson, D. 1993. Shorebirds of the Pacific Northwest. University of Washington and Seattle Audubon Society.

Paulson, D. 1995. Summary report of the Washington Bird Records Committee. *WOS News*, Washington Ornithological Society, December, 1995.

Peterson, A. 1995. Erroneous party-hour data and a proposed method of correcting observer effort in Christmas Bird Counts. *Journal of Field Ornithology* 66(3): 385-90.

Powers, L. 1996. Wintering Sharp-shinned Hawks (*Accipiter striatus*) in an urban area of southwestern Idaho. *Northwestern Naturalist* 77: 9.

Roberts, H. 1992. Birds of East-Central Idaho.

Root, Terry. 1988. Atlas of wintering North American birds: an analysis of Christmas Bird Count data. University of Chicago Press.

Sanger, G. 1965. Observations of wildlife off the coast of Washington and Oregon in 1963, with notes on the Laysan Albatross. *Murrelet* 46)1): 1.

Sanger, G. 1970. The seasonal distribution of some seabirds off Washington and Oregon with notes on their ecology and behavior. *Condor* 72(3): 339-357.

Sanger, G. 1972. Checklist of bird observations from the eastern North Pacific Ocean. *Murrelet* 53(2): 16.

Sanger, G. 1974. Black-footed Albatross and Laysan Albatross, *in* King, W., ed., Pelagic Studies of Seabirds in the Central and Eastern Pacific Ocean. Smithsonian Contributions to Zoology No. 158.

Sauer, J. R. and S. Droege. (eds.) 1990. Survey designs and statistical methods for the estimation of avian population trends. U. S. Fish Wildl. Serv. Biol. Rep. 90(1).

Scott, J.M. and H. Nehls. 1974. First Oregon records for Thick-billed Murre. *Western Birds* 5: 137.

Schmidt, O. 1989. Rare Birds of Oregon. Oregon Field Ornithologists Special Publication No. 5.

Smith, K. 1979. The effect of weather, people and time on 12 Christmas Bird Counts, 1954-1973. *American Birds* 33(4): 698-702.

Stephens, D. and S. Sturts. 1991. Idaho Bird Distribution. Special Publication No. 11, Idaho Museum of Natural History.

Sturts, S. 1993. Birds and Birding Routes of the Idaho Panhandle. Idaho Department of Fish and Game.

Summers, S. 1993. A Birder's Guide to the Klamath Basin. Klamath Basin Audubon Society.

Taylor, D. and C. Trost. 1987. The status of rare birds in Idaho. *Murrelet* 68:69.

Tweit, B. and J. Skriletz. 1996. Second report of the Washington Bird Records Committee. *Washington Birds* 5: 7-28.

Wahl, T., K. Morgan and K. Vermeer. 1993. Seabird distribution off British Columbia and Washington, *in* Vermeer, K., K. Briggs, K. Morgan and D. Siegel-Causey, eds. The status, ecology and conservation of marine birds of the North Pacific. Canadian Wildlife Service Special Publication, Ottawa.

Wahl, T. 1995. Birds of Whatcom County: Status and distribution. Published by T. R. Wahl, Bellingham, Washington.

Weber, W., and E. Hunn. 1978. First record of the Little Blue Heron for British Columbia and Washington. *Western Birds* 9: 33.

Index